Provides a fresh and innovative approach to designing and implementing your cybersecurity awareness program. Unlike the majority of books on the subject, the language is easy to digest and the techniques human-focused. I would recommend this book to anyone involved in information security looking to engage the wider organisation and improve cybersecurity awareness.

Helen Mary Jones CITP CISSP, *Group Information Security Manager, The Jockey Club*

A must read for all CISOs and information security leaders and people that engage people into their cybersecurity strategy. This book has made me realise that our traditional methods to cybersecurity awareness, behaviour and culture has needed a substantial modern approach to empowering people into being a strong link in cybersecurity.

Joseph Carson CISSP, *Chief Security Scientist and Advisory CISO, Thycotic*

A book about information security awareness, behaviours and cultures, by people who live and breathe all three. *Cybersecurity ABCs* explores new depths, debunks myths, answers questions and shines a light on what it means to truly address the all-important human-related elements of modern security. The perfect guide for any security leader looking to make their people their strongest security asset.

Michael Hill, Editor, *Infosecurity Magazine*

An excellent read, and essential for cybersecurity leaders at all levels. This book provides not only easy to understand language, but 'lived' experiences, techniques and considerations to improve awareness, behaviour and culture within an organisation. It provides a holistic approach, starting with examining the behaviour of the cybersecurity professional, before dealing with wider organisational change. As this is the only resource I have seen to offer practical awareness solutions, it also makes it the missing piece from most major, industry-leading certifications.

Gary Cocklin CITP CISSP, *Senior Cybersecurity Instructor, UK Royal Air Force (RAF)*

This book does what every great business book does – it makes you think (differently, laterally, objectively), and helps develop those thoughts into structure. It doesn't provide an ordered checklist, but rather, architects a challenge or puzzle for each reader to solve. All of the clues, tools and techniques are laid out by the authors for each of us to successfully build a solution that is a right fit for our working environment.

Richard Nealon, *Trustee of The SABSA Institute*

The perfect read for anyone looking to develop their understanding of the human side of cybersecurity. Trying to create meaningful awareness and driving positive changes in behaviour for those who don't live and breathe cybersecurity is a huge challenge that every organisation faces. While there is no magic switch to create a positive cybersecurity culture, using this book as a tool will certainly provide you with the best knowledge, practical tips and insights to help you change the direction of your journey today.

Joe Pettit, *Director, Bora*

Cybersecurity and psychology make great bed fellows. Digging into awareness, behaviour and culture, the authors address the underlying 'why' that is key to engagement and empowering employees. A pragmatism gained in the field is evident throughout the book making *Cybersecurity ABCs* a comprehensive manual for the industry professional, that is rich in research and practical advice.

Andrea Manning, *Founder and CEO, CyberPie*

This deeply-researched discussion of the human side of cybersecurity presents clear and actionable guidance on building a robust security programme that gives employees the knowledge and tools to be the first and best line of defence against cyber threats. The authors draw from their extensive professional experience and academic research to explain techniques for raising awareness, encouraging positive behaviours, and building a corporate culture in which protecting against cyber threats becomes as easy and as natural for the entire workforce as reciting the ABCs. I highly recommend it for anyone with an interest in cybersecurity.

Donald Edwards CISSP, *Director of Network Security, Salesforce*

Cybersecurity ABCs sparked so many creative ideas for my role in awareness and training, I had to stop reading to go chat to my team about the suggested actions in how to make our awareness program and security culture at HPE more effective and mature.

Joanne O'Connor, *Cybersecurity Training Program Manager, HPE*

This book is extremely important because we tend to focus too much on technology. But as we have seen, a lot of security incidents are not prevented by technology but through awareness, behaviour and culture. What is also really uplifting is to read a book which is not designed for technical people but instead empowers everyday IT-users to help build security and take part in the day to day IT-security work.

David Jacoby, *Security Evangelist and Researcher, Kaspersky*

CYBERSECURITY ABCs

BCS, THE CHARTERED INSTITUTE FOR IT

BCS, The Chartered Institute for IT, is committed to making IT good for society. We use the power of our network to bring about positive, tangible change. We champion the global IT profession and the interests of individuals, engaged in that profession, for the benefit of all.

Exchanging IT expertise and knowledge
The Institute fosters links between experts from industry, academia and business to promote new thinking, education and knowledge sharing.

Supporting practitioners
Through continuing professional development and a series of respected IT qualifications, the Institute seeks to promote professional practice tuned to the demands of business. It provides practical support and information services to its members and volunteer communities around the world.

Setting standards and frameworks
The Institute collaborates with government, industry and relevant bodies to establish good working practices, codes of conduct, skills frameworks and common standards. It also offers a range of consultancy services to employers to help them adopt best practice.

Become a member
Over 70,000 people including students, teachers, professionals and practitioners enjoy the benefits of BCS membership. These include access to an international community, invitations to a roster of local and national events, career development tools and a quarterly thought-leadership magazine. Visit www.bcs.org/membership to find out more.

Further information
BCS, The Chartered Institute for IT,
3 Newbridge Square,
Swindon, SN1 1BY, United Kingdom.
T +44 (0) 1793 417 417
(Monday to Friday, 09:00 to 17:00 UK time)
www.bcs.org/contact
http://shop.bcs.org/

CYBERSECURITY ABCs
Delivering awareness, behaviours and culture change

Jessica Barker, Adrian Davis, Bruce Hallas and
Ciarán Mc Mahon

Published by BCS Learning and Development Ltd, a wholly owned subsidiary of BCS, The Chartered Institute for IT, 3 Newbridge Square, Swindon, SN1 1BY, UK.
www.bcs.org

Paperback ISBN: 978-1-78017-4242
PDF ISBN: 978-1-78017-4259
ePUB ISBN: 978-1-78017-4266
Kindle ISBN: 978-1-78017-4273

Ebook available

British Cataloguing in Publication Data.
A CIP catalogue record for this book is available at the British Library.

Disclaimer:
The views expressed in this book are of the authors and do not necessarily reflect the views of the Institute or BCS Learning and Development Ltd except where explicitly stated as such. Although every care has been taken by the authors and BCS Learning and Development Ltd in the preparation of the publication, no warranty is given by the authors or BCS Learning and Development Ltd as publisher as to the accuracy or completeness of the information contained within it and neither the authors nor BCS Learning and Development Ltd shall be responsible or liable for any loss or damage whatsoever arising by virtue of such information or any instructions or advice contained within this publication or by any of the aforementioned.

Publisher's acknowledgements
Reviewers: Heather Taylor and Sema Yuce
Publisher: Ian Borthwick
Commissioning editor: Rebecca Youé
Production manager: Florence Leroy
Project manager: Sunrise Setting Ltd
Copy-editor: Gillian Bourn
Proofreader: Barbara Eastman
Indexer: Matthew Gale
Cover design: Alex Wright
Cover image: Shutterstock_172537049_donvictorio
Typeset by Lapiz Digital Services, Chennai, India
Printed by Hobbs the Printers Ltd, Totton, Hampshire, UK

CONTENTS

LIST OF FIGURES AND TABLES

FIGURES

TABLES

AUTHORS

Jessica Barker is an award-winning global leader in the human side of cybersecurity. She is co-founder and co-CEO of Cygenta, where she follows her passion of positively influencing cybersecurity awareness, behaviour and culture in organisations around the world. She has delivered face-to-face cybersecurity awareness sessions to over 35,000 people in over 23 countries. Jessica has been named one of the top 20 most influential women in cybersecurity in the UK and is the Chair of ClubCISO. She is a popular keynote speaker, including keynoting RSA San Francisco in 2020. Jessica is the go-to cybersecurity expert for many media outlets, appearing on BBC News, Sky News, Channel 4 News, BBC radio and much more. In September 2020, Jessica's book *Confident Cybersecurity* was published by Kogan Page and became a number one Amazon bestseller within hours of publication.

Adrian Davis. With a career spanning over 20 years, Adrian has worked across many sectors from defence to entertainment as a cybersecurity, supply chain and programme/operations management expert. Currently the CEO of IAAC (Information Assurance Advisory Council), he has significant senior commercial and strategic experience gained by leading the Europe, Middle East and Africa region for a global cybersecurity membership organisation; leading and creating multi-disciplinary sales, technology and consulting teams; and managing a consulting business delivering cybersecurity projects to blue-chip organisations globally. He is an acknowledged leader in information security, a published author and a writer of international information security standards. He holds a BSc(Hons) and a PhD from the University of London; a Durham University MBA; the CISSP; an FBCS CITP; and a Visiting Professorship at the University of Sunderland within the Faculty of Computer Science.

Bruce Hallas is the founder at Re-thinking the Human Factor. He is widely recognised, by practitioners through to regulators, as making a significant contribution to re-assessing the opportunity for improving employee awareness, behaviour and culture. Through a combination of his hugely successful Re-thinking the Human Factor podcast, the accompanying book and his coaching and training programmes, he has contributed to reshaping how senior information security and privacy professionals manage the risk associated with human factor. His insights are the outcome of a long-standing commitment to research and the experience of implementing these findings within organisations and work forces across the world. As the challenge of raising awareness, influencing behaviour and embedding values and practices into culture are not unique to security and privacy, much of what he shares originates from outside of the security and privacy industry. In some respects, Bruce is seen as a curator of insights as much as an innovator in how they can be applied, within the context of security and privacy. The appeal of Bruce's work is in how he introduces you to a better understanding of what it means to be human and then uses this to highlight what aspects of these insights contribute to improved awareness, behaviour and culture. He has then used these insights to produce a range of design principles which form the basis for his 'Design with the Human in Mind' philosophy. He has then combined these design principles, with 20 years' experience in information security and privacy, to create the SABC® framework which integrates fully into any management system. The framework supports security and privacy professionals, to help them deliver change programmes which address the limitations of traditional education and awareness programmes. Bruce's practical and science-based insights, and his ability to draw on real life examples that almost everyone can relate to, have meant he has become a sought-after specialist around the world. He supports CISOs, DPOs and Education and Awareness Managers, to reset their strategic vision and build the capacity to achieve this, whilst ultimately being able to stand up to the highest levels of public and private scrutiny should they ever suffer a security or privacy incident.

Ciarán Mc Mahon is a director of the Institute of Cyber Security and an award-winning historian and philosopher of psychology. Ciarán is the author of the critically acclaimed *The Psychology of Social Media* (Routledge), and editor of the forthcoming *Psychological Insights for Understanding COVID-19 and Media and Technology* (Routledge). Ciarán's research interests lie at the intersection of psychology and technology, specifically cybersecurity and social media. He is an occasional lecturer at the School of Psychology, University College Dublin and a regular tweeter at @cjamcmahon. A former Government of Ireland Scholar, Ciarán has published peer-reviewed research on the history of psychological language, the psychology of social media, the social impact of cybercrime, digital wellness and human factors in cybersecurity. Ciarán has extensive media experience and regularly contributes to international media including *Wired*, Sky News, BBC World Service, Business Insider, *USA Today*, *Fortune Magazine* and *The Guardian*. A compelling public speaker, Ciarán is a passionate advocate for public engagement with online safety and cybersecurity.

ABBREVIATIONS

(ISC)²	International Information Systems Security Certification Consortium (www.isc2.org)
2FA	two-factor authentication
AIDA	awareness, interest, desire and action
B2B	business to business
B2C	business to consumers
BYOD	bring your own device (or, to security professionals, bring your own disaster)
CBT	computer-based training
CEO	chief executive officer
CISM	Certified Information Security Manager – a credential issued by ISACA
CISO	chief information security officer
CISSP	Certified Information Systems Security Professional – a credential issued by (ISC)²
COVID-19	coronavirus disease (https://www.who.int/emergencies/diseases/novel-coronavirus-2019/technical-guidance/naming-the-coronavirus-disease-(covid-2019)-and-the-virus-that-causes-it)
DNA	deoxyribonucleic acid
FCA	Financial Conduct Authority (UK)
FUD	fear, uncertainty and doubt
GDPR	European Union General Data Protection Regulation (properly: Regulation (EU) 2016/679 of the European Parliament and of the Council of 27 April 2016 on the protection of natural persons with regard to the processing of personal data and on the free movement of such data, and repealing Directive 95/46/EC (General Data Protection Regulation))
HARK	Hypothesizing After the Results are Known
HR	human resources
HTML	Hypertext Markup Language
IBM	International Business Machines, now just IBM (nicknamed 'Big Blue')

IEC	International Electrotechnical Commission (www.iec.ch)
ISACA	Originally Information Systems Audit and Control Association, now just ISACA (www.isaca.org)
ISF	Information Security Forum (www.securityforum.org)
ISO	International Organization for Standardization (www.iso.org)
IT	information technology
KPI	key performance indicator
MAS	Monetary Authority of Singapore (Singapore)
NCSC	National Cyber Security Centre (UK, www.ncsc.gov.uk)
NHS	National Health Service (UK)
NIST	National Institute of Standards and Technology (US, www.nist.gov)
PCI DSS	Payment Card Industry Data Security Standard (https://www.pcisecuritystandards.org/)
RSA	Rivest, Shamir and Adleman (www.rsaconference.com)
SANS	SysAdmin, Audit, Network and Security (www.sans.org)
SAS	Scandinavian Air Systems
SMART	specific, measurable, achievable, relevant (or realistic) and time-bound
SP	Special Publication – used by NIST (q.v.)
URL	Uniform Resource Locator (web address)
USB	Universal Serial Bus
VPN	virtual private network
Wi-Fi	Wireless Fidelity

GLOSSARY

Availability heuristic: The tendency of an individual relies on immediate examples that come to a given person's mind when evaluating a specific topic, concept, method or decision.[1]

Awareness: Focuses attention on security.[2]

Business email compromise (BEC): A form of phishing attack where a criminal attempts to trick a senior executive (or budget holder) into transferring funds, or revealing sensitive information.[3]

Choice architecture: Organizing the context in which people make decisions.[4]

Cognitive dissonance: Cognitive dissonance is a term for the state of discomfort felt when two or more modes of thought contradict each other. The clashing cognitions may include ideas, beliefs, or the knowledge that one has behaved in a certain way.[5]

Cybersecurity: 1. 'Cyberspace security'; preservation of confidentiality, integrity and availability of information in the Cyberspace.[6,7] 2. The state of being protected against the criminal or unauthorized use of electronic data, or the measures taken to achieve this.[8]

Cybersecurity awareness: Focusing individuals' attention on protecting against the criminal or unauthorised use of electronic data, so that they can respond accordingly.[9]

Cyberspace: Complex environment resulting from the interaction of people, software and services on the Internet by means of technology devices and networks connected to it, which does not exist in any physical form.[10]

Double-blind experiment: An experiment in which neither the participant nor the person gathering the dependent variable data knows which group the participant is in.[11]

Dunning–Kruger effect: People tend to hold overly favourable views of their abilities in many social and intellectual domains.[12]

Gamification: The practice of making activities more like games in order to make them more interesting or enjoyable.[13]

HARK(ing): Presenting a post hoc hypothesis in the introduction of a research report as if it were an a priori hypothesis.[14]

Hawthorne effect: The phenomenon that employees perform better when they feel singled out for attention or feel that management is concerned about their welfare.[15]

Heuristic: A mental shortcut that allows an individual to make a decision, pass judgment, or solve a problem quickly and with minimal mental effort.[16]

Norm: An accepted standard or a way of behaving or doing things that most people agree with.[17]

Normalcy bias: The tendency of an individual to disbelieve or minimize threat warnings.[18]

Nudge: An aspect of the choice architecture that alters people's behaviour in a predictable way without forbidding any options or significantly changing their economic incentives.[19]

Null hypothesis: The statement postulating an experiment will find no variations between the control and experimental states, which is, no union between variants. Statistical tests are rendered to experimental outcomes in effort to disprove or refute the previously established significance level.[20]

Operant conditioning: A method of learning where the consequences of a response determine the probability of the response being repeated.[21]

Pedagogy: The study of the methods and activities of teaching.[22]

Phishing: Fraudulent process of attempting to acquire private or confidential information by masquerading as a trustworthy entity in an electronic communication.[23]

Planned behaviour theory: Predict an individual's intention to engage in a behaviour at a specific time and place. The theory was intended to explain all behaviours over which people have the ability to exert self-control.[24]

Protection motivation theory: Describes how individuals are motivated to react in a self-protective way towards a health threat. It has four key elements: 'threat appraisal', followed by 'coping appraisal', which comprises 'response efficacy' – the belief that certain processes will mitigate the threat – and 'self-efficacy', an individual's idea of their own ability to implement the required actions to mitigate the threat.[25]

Ransomware: A type of malware (like Viruses, Trojans, etc.) that infect the computer systems of users and manipulates the infected system in a way, that the victim cannot (partially or fully) use it and the data stored on it. The victim usually shortly after receives a blackmail note by pop-up, pressing the victim to pay a ransom (hence the name) to regain full access to system and files.[26]

Salience (or saliency) bias: The tendency of an individual to focus on items or information that are more noteworthy while ignoring those that do not grab our attention.[27]

Self-efficacy (theory): The belief in one's capabilities to organize and execute the courses of action required to manage prospective situations.[28]

Social proof: The phenomenon of people modelling their behaviour based on how they see others behave.[29]

Spear phishing: Spear phishing is a more sophisticated and elaborate version of phishing. It targets specific organisations or individuals, and seeks unauthorized access to confidential data. Just like in standard phishing, spear phishing attacks impersonate trusted sources. Moreover the attacks are personalised, and tactics such as sender impersonation are used.[30]

Training: Produces relevant and needed security skills and competencies by practitioners of functional specialties.[31]

Two-factor authentication: Two-step verification (sometimes called two-factor authentication or 2FA) is a more secure solution than just passwords. It works by requiring two different methods to authenticate yourself.[32]

PREFACE

Having been very fortunate to see all three of my co-authors speak at various events – separately – I was even more fortunate when they not only agreed to speak at the events I was involved with, but then agreed to collaborate on a wild idea of mine. *Cybersecurity ABCs* is the fruit of that collaboration.

The *Cybersecurity ABCs* started from my dissatisfaction at security awareness. I have sat on many sides of the awareness fence: a consumer of security awareness programmes; a creator of security awareness programmes; and a consultant offering guidance on creating and running such programmes. I have also attended many talks and presentations on security awareness and related technologies. What has always struck me is the lack of success despite all the effort put into awareness programmes – and the cybersecurity profession's resignation to failure.

So, rather than invoke the quote attributed to Einstein that 'insanity is doing the same thing over and over again and expecting different results', I called Jessica, Ciarán and Bruce and I asked them if they could bring their unique perspectives together and create a new approach to security awareness – one that actually made a difference. Luckily, they said yes. What I didn't tell them at the time was that they would be responsible for writing and delivering a set of workshops!

The genesis of the book came from a series of workshops held by International Information Systems Security Certification Consortium (www.isc2.org) (ISC)² across Europe, Middle East and Africa in 2016–2018, where Jessica, Ciarán and Bruce ran half-day sessions with information security professionals. It was clear to us both before these sessions and after that there was a demand for new approaches and new thinking in the field of security awareness. What we didn't realise was the demand for radical thinking from industry professionals. The perspective offered – that integrating awareness with behaviour change and using both of these approaches to reinforce or produce a security culture would yield tangible positive outcomes – was extremely well received by audiences everywhere we ran the workshops. We realised soon afterwards that we needed to capture our knowledge, experiences as well as our thoughts and learnings from the workshops – and hence this book was born.

This book is testament to what happens when you put very experienced and intelligent people in a room and leave them to their own devices. It has been and remains a pleasure to work with my co-authors, whether remotely or face to face. *Cybersecurity ABCs* owes its richness and rigour to Jessica, Ciarán and Bruce and their unselfish sharing of knowledge and experience.

Adrian Davis

1 SECURITY AWARENESS: A PERENNIAL CHALLENGE

Adrian Davis

The topic of security awareness has exercised academics and practitioners for well over 20 years. A search for articles on 'information security awareness' and 'cybersecurity awareness' using Google Scholar, for example, yields over 3,300,000 results at the time of writing,[33] while an Amazon search presents over 200 books. International and national standards such as ISO/IEC 27001, ISO/IEC 27021, NIST SP 800-50 and proprietary standards such as the ISF Standard of Good Practice and ISACA COBIT 5 for information security, devote all or part of their contents to cybersecurity awareness and associated material. Innumerable presentations have been given on the topic by practitioners, academics and consultants; and there is a thriving industry offering awareness programmes, content, guidance on running programmes, and tools to help the cybersecurity professional deliver better programmes, better content and achieve the hoped-for results.

And of course, this outpouring of research, literature, knowledge and experience is still growing. So, why add to this voluminous collection of knowledge?

Simply, we believe there is a way to do things much better. Rather than focus on awareness on its own, we believe that a different approach is needed. We call that different approach the ABCs. Our approach links awareness, behaviour and culture together, so that each reinforces the other: awareness campaigns are designed to change behaviour for the better; better behaviour translates into cultural norms; cultural norms maintain awareness and set expected behaviours.

WHERE ARE WE TODAY?

Despite the outpouring of knowledge and expertise, and the efforts and resources expended on security awareness, the general perception is that cybersecurity awareness is, to a great extent, not delivering. The desired objectives, for example that employees will 'think security' or that a security culture will be created, are rarely, if ever, achieved. Instead it still seems as though individuals frequently click on malicious links in emails, more incidents occur or the security professional is pushed further away from the business. The timing of awareness programmes, often delivered when people join and then refreshed annually, seem to militate against building understanding and commitment to cybersecurity and are often submerged under day-to-day issues, change programmes and all the demands on an individual's time at work. There is also the issue of getting time in front of employees – an awareness programme has to slot into the schedule of corporate events, communications and training. Unfortunately, as many cybersecurity professionals can attest, cybersecurity is placed low on the list, behind many other corporate communications.

But how did we get here? Why, despite all the money, time and brainpower thrown at security awareness, are we still seeing the same problems and results?

There are probably as many reasons as there are stars in the sky, but there are several that seem to crop up time and time again, which are:

- myths of awareness;
- unclear objectives;
- delivery;
- problem exists between chair and keyboard;
- focusing on ourselves alone.

In this chapter we'll examine each of these reasons in turn.

MYTHS OF AWARENESS

There are many myths about cybersecurity awareness. The top five are listed below:

1. Cybersecurity is everyone's responsibility.
2. Cybersecurity is important to employees.
3. Cybersecurity awareness will turn everyone into a 'human firewall'.
4. Cybersecurity awareness will make everyone behave in the way we want.
5. Cybersecurity awareness will turn into a security culture.

Let's start exploding these myths with number one in our list. Unfortunately, information security, despite what we think as cybersecurity professionals, isn't everyone's responsibility. For most organisations, it's the responsibility of the security team, in the same way that invoices and payments are the responsibility of the finance team. If it was the employees' responsibility, then they would have been employed to do cybersecurity – not the position they currently hold.

There is also the perception that the information employees use in their jobs is the organisation's information, not **their** information, so protecting it isn't their problem: it's the organisation's responsibility to protect it.

The second myth is that cybersecurity is important to employees. As has been repeatedly demonstrated, employees are happy to give their work password for a chocolate bar;[34] sell information from their current employer for quite small sums; or use their corporate email to create accounts and login to dating (and other, ahem, interesting) sites.[35] Getting through the day, their daily tasks, getting paid, getting promoted, getting recognised and thanked are all much, much more important to employees than not clicking on suspicious looking links or checking email meta-data. Of course, cybersecurity is important to us; that could be why we do the jobs we do, but for the vast majority of people cybersecurity is low on the list of priorities and interests. There have been attempts to link cybersecurity to staff performance reviews and bonuses, to spur interest and attention. The jury is still out on these initiatives: at issue is how little cybersecurity can be linked to business performance and, of course, finding fault and tracing business impact back to an individual.

The term 'human firewall' has become very popular and is used by a number of security companies at the time of writing. No doubt the term will pass out of favour and be replaced by something similar. Our third myth, regardless of the words, is that once employees have received their cybersecurity awareness training, they will return to their desks and devices and stop everything that looks like a phishing email, dodgy attachment or piece of malware (never mind that real firewalls don't always stop such traffic). Training of any sort confers a 'halo effect' and people go back to work keen and full of good intentions, which are then lost as the daily grind of meetings, emails and work-related activities resumes. Even with reminders and follow-ups, the impact of the training is lost. So, our human firewalls – although I'm not sure people would like to be labelled as such – may start with the best of intentions but over time their effectiveness lessens and can return to pre-training levels.

Our penultimate myth is that awareness can change behaviour and make everyone behave in the way we want or behave just as we cybersecurity professionals do. Many organisations expect certain patterns of behaviour (and actively encourage employees to align with those expectations) and, if the desired cybersecurity behaviours are discordant, then they will be ignored and rejected.

> On the other hand, we should also be mindful that we don't want everyone to become suspicious, mistrustful and paranoid of every single email or website, believe that every attachment is malicious, nor do we want everyone in the organisation to 'think like a hacker'; if nothing else, the helpdesk could be inundated!

The last myth is that we can create a security culture by awareness alone. Roughly defined, culture is 'the way we do things around here' and is made up of many factors. I like the cultural web (Johnson et al., 2012), which highlights the importance of six factors in creating or reinforcing a culture. The cultural web, simply, indicates that many factors influence and shape culture. Each factor, on its own or in concert with others, can influence the culture and can contribute to maintaining that culture as well. The six factors are:

1. stories and myths;
2. rituals and routines;
3. symbols;
4. organisational structure;
5. control systems;
6. power structures.

This is not the only model of culture – Geert Hofstede and his collaborators have for many years looked at culture across and in multinational organisations and produced some very insightful findings (see Hofstede et al., 2002, 2010).[36] What the cultural web neatly illustrates is that culture is made up of many interrelated and interlocking factors and that they may have to be addressed simultaneously to start the process of changing or building a culture.

An organisation will often have more than one culture; sometimes these are cultures influenced by location, by professional or commercial grouping or by technical expertise. Good examples are the difference between sales and finance functions, or US and European offices. Each of these cultures is built up over time and reinforced by the people who work in those cultures. Culture is 'sticky' in that as people join a company, they are exposed to that culture and start to behave in a manner the culture and people expect. That's why changing culture is often so difficult – it requires people to change their mindset and their behaviours. The reason why we need to explode this myth is that culture change and a security culture will not spring into existence because of a set of phishing emails or a couple of hours of awareness training a year: it requires much more than this.

While we have the eventual aim of creating a security culture, we should consider how we can build towards that goal. That means we have to revise our objectives and ask ourselves a simple question: 'what are we trying to achieve?', which is the next topic we cover.

WHAT ARE WE TRYING TO ACHIEVE?

Take a step back and think about your latest awareness programme. What were you trying to achieve? What did you want the programme to achieve? What did your boss want the programme to achieve?

We need to go further back than this and understand what we mean by awareness. All too often, we don't present an awareness programme; we present a mix of awareness, training and education, dressed up as 'awareness'. Confusing these three terms – awareness, training and education – and their objectives means that a clear message or path to understanding can be obscured or lost, making the whole exercise deeply unsatisfying for all concerned.

So, let's start out by defining these three terms, using NIST SP800-16 and SP 800-50 as a basis.

Awareness

Security awareness efforts are designed to change behaviour or reinforce good security practices. Awareness is defined in US National Institute of Standards and Technology (NIST) Special Publication 800-16[44] as follows:

> Awareness is not training. The purpose of awareness presentations is simply to focus attention on security. Awareness presentations are intended to allow individuals to recognize IT security concerns and respond accordingly.

In awareness activities, the learner is the recipient of information [...] Awareness relies on reaching broad audiences with attractive packaging techniques.

Training

Training is defined in NIST Special Publication 800-16 as follows:

The 'Training' level of the learning continuum strives to produce relevant and needed security skills and competencies by practitioners of functional specialties.

The most significant difference between training and awareness is that training seeks to teach skills, which allow a person to perform a specific function, while awareness seeks to focus an individual's attention on an issue or set of issues. The skills acquired during training are built upon the awareness foundation, in particular, upon the security basics and literacy material. A training curriculum may not necessarily lead to a formal degree from an institution of higher learning; however, a training course may contain much of the same material found in a course that a college or university includes in a certificate or degree programme.

Education

Education is defined in NIST Special Publication 800-16 as follows:

The 'Education' level integrates all of the security skills and competencies of the various functional specialties into a common body of knowledge, adds a multidisciplinary study of concepts, issues, and principles (technological and social), and strives to produce IT security specialists and professionals capable of vision and pro-active response.

Balancing awareness, training and education

Once you see the definitions in black and white, it is obvious that the three terms are very different and require different approaches for success. They also have different outcomes. However, the three are readily and easily confused – by vendors advertising awareness programmes that are training programmes based on their content for example – and by cybersecurity professionals.

Such confusion results in mixed messages, poor management of expectations and, eventually, poor outcomes. To help fix these terms in the readers' mind and understand what each approach is capable of delivering, Table 1.1 is offered as guidance.

This table can help guide our thinking and provide a tool to integrate the various approaches. If we think about phishing campaigns for example, they are a mix of awareness – telling people that emails may be harmful and that emails are used for fraud, theft and so on – and a mix of training – getting people to click on 'report phishing buttons' or not to click on links. The clicking on the 'report phishing button' is a specific function that people are taught; nothing else. Getting the blend right between awareness and training is vital, as it equips people with the relevant knowledge, response and, where required, the specific action to take.

Table 1.1 Defining awareness, training and education

Approach	Audience	Key objective	Outcome
Awareness	Passive	Focus attention on security	Recognise information technology (IT) security concerns and respond accordingly
Training	Active	Build knowledge and skills to facilitate job performance	Teach skills that allow a person to perform a specific function
Education	Very active	Integrate all of the security skills and competencies of the various functional specialities into a common body of knowledge	Produce IT security specialists and professionals capable of vision and proactive response

Awareness is often treated as a means to an end but for it to be most effective, it should form part of something bigger. Making people aware of an issue isn't a call to action, nor does it tell them what to do, as described above. To make awareness work, it should lead on to further activities, as shown in the engagement journey, namely, promote understanding, increase engagement and support action, as shown in Figure 1.1.

Figure 1.1 The engagement journey

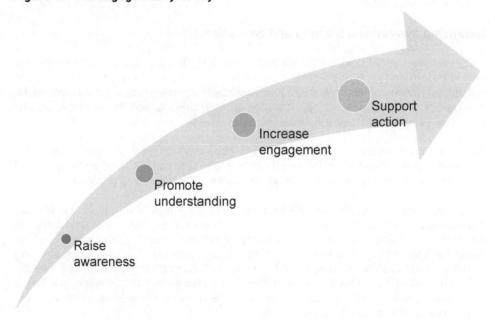

Moving from raising awareness to supporting action will take time and will require the use of different skills and communication methods. If we look at the engagement journey, the start is the first step of raising awareness. That can be achieved by a simple conversation, a short video or even a message on a mouse mat. Raising awareness will typically be aimed at as large an audience as possible and will typically use 'push' or one-way forms of communication such as videos, lectures, online training and physical media. Next comes the harder step, that of promoting understanding. It's easy to make someone aware of something but actually making them interested, willing to engage and spend time understanding what they are being told is harder. Typically, the audience size reduces as the effort required to promote understanding can be significant to reach a large audience. This step may involve regular presentations to groups by the security function, hands on demonstrations and follow-up. Once the audience reaches an understanding, then the programme needs to keep people engaged and interested. This is the point where the audience should be actively doing something, asking questions and even conducting simple tasks with supervision. Seminars, workshops and detailed briefings will be the tools of choice. Finally, the objective will be to get the audience to support cybersecurity actions and take an active part in making those actions happen.

Awareness, while covering the majority of people in an organisation, is one part of the equation. While it's true that organisations will not seek to train or educate many individuals – nor could they within the typical budget provided – there is a place for identifying individuals or functions where the more in-depth approach of training or education could provide benefit. Education is often focused on particular individuals and on information security, for example through the application of professional certifications such as Certified Information Systems Security Professional (CISSP) and Certified Information Security Manager (CISM) or academic qualifications such as undergraduate and postgraduate degrees. This level of education can prepare individuals for promotions or allow them to gain further insight and raise their value to the security function and the organisation. Training can be extended to a wider group of individuals – a good example is training user access administrators to add user rights according to a security policy and procedure – thus ensuring that a consistent, secure approach is followed.

Ideally, taking into consideration all the constraints in an organisation, a balance between awareness, training and education should be struck. All cost time and money; all have particular benefits. Awareness is a 'marathon, not a sprint' and requires frequent repetition, is difficult to measure and yields the least obvious results, yet it is vital that individuals in an organisation have a basic comprehension of cybersecurity and the function. Training can be a one-off, can be measured (relatively) easily and can yield results quickly, while education may yield results over the longer term.

Building on our understanding of awareness, training and education, we can start to examine how we can deliver each of these to our audiences, which is covered next.

DELIVERY

When we think about how cybersecurity awareness is delivered, it's often lumped in with IT or compliance subjects; through 'merch' (merchandise) – posters, cups, mouse mats and so on; often delivered as part of induction programmes (if such things exist); delivered as part of annual computer-based training (CBT) or via an 'awareness programme'; on the intranet (as a microsite maybe, with downloads and videos); and included in newsletters. There is, of course, also the face-to-face delivery in a meeting, or over the phone when someone calls asking for help. Let's briefly review the mechanisms of delivery and highlight some important features of each.

Annual training

The first delivery mechanism we touch on is the annual ritual of training and the incorporation of cybersecurity into that training round. In some industry verticals, staff have to undergo some form of annual training to carry on with their jobs. It is often seen as a good idea to bundle the annual mandatory training and topics such anti-money laundering, compliance and cybersecurity together. From one perspective, it means that everyone does the training (it's mandatory), the completion of the training and any associated tests are recorded (so it can be proved that everyone has done the mandatory training) and it means that time doesn't have to be found at other points during the year to run cybersecurity awareness workshops. From another perspective (that of the employee), it's another course to get through as fast as possible in order to get back to the real work. Typically, little or no time is set aside to do these courses, nor is there any visible reward for completion. Even if there is a test at the end of the course, it's a hurdle to get past, not a learning opportunity. Stories of interns completing training on behalf of staff members, or one person doing the course and then sharing the questions and answers with the team, which reduce the reach and impact of the training, are rife. Even if face-to-face training is used, it can be very hard to judge or accurately measure the impact, value or long-term benefit of that training.

Associated with this delivery mechanism is the awareness campaign, where a theme is chosen and then presentations, emails, articles and training are all bundled together and then distributed to staff over a period of time.

Merch

Traditional security awareness relies on 'merch', combined with some form of awareness programme, lecture or other training (e.g. CBT).

> I remember seeing a poster in an office toilet[45] in Norway (yes, really) that had an image of a toothbrush and the Norwegian equivalent of 'you wouldn't reuse this, so why reuse your password?'

There have been cups, coffee mugs, mouse mats and pencils, all with messages such as 'Think security', 'Think, don't click' in organisational circulation and these are probably still doing the rounds in organisations today. Screensavers with such messages used to be popular as well. These are all **passive** methods of communicating – they all depend on an individual reading the slogans and then doing something – or being engaged enough to even take notice of the message. Unfortunately, employees can also become desensitised to these images and slogans, which further limit the impact and usefulness of merch.

New starter induction

Next comes new starter induction. Larger organisations can afford the luxury of a full day to orient staff but, even then, cybersecurity may be covered in only one or two slides. Typically, those slides won't be delivered by a cybersecurity professional, so the messages need to be clear and succinct. The messages often get buried among all the other important things the new staff member has been told. And, of course, from day one the new staff member is starting to learn the culture. While large organisations can induct their staff, smaller organisations often can't, so the new staff member learns on the job. Typically, the new staff member will learn from their peers and colleagues, so they will be further indoctrinated into the prevailing culture. In fact, it's hard to escape the reality that most training really does happen on the job, day to day; and much of the learning happens by a process of observation. Some organisations have gone so far as to deliberately state that staff will learn by '80 per cent experience, 20 per cent training'.

Computer-based training

CBT ranges from the genuinely impressive to downright awful. Videos, stills and voiceovers all have their uses but they have to be done in the same style and with the same high quality. There is nothing worse than a mix of high- and low-quality images, bad voiceovers or inconsistent styles: all detract from the messages the CBT is trying to deliver. An effective CBT can attempt to tell a story, preferably one to which staff can relate, that highlights key decision points and the impact of the decisions taken. These decisions can then be referred back to what should have been done, the questions that should have been asked and the behaviour or policies that should have been followed. However, not all CBT follows this approach and is often slide-based regurgitations of policy statements, snippets from standards and quotes from laws or regulation, followed by a test. Hardly stirring stuff.

There has been an industry-wide trend to use phishing campaigns to train and educate users as a form of CBT to raise awareness. The majority of CBT tools for this are sophisticated, allowing multiple campaigns to be run, identification of repeat 'offenders' and even instant feedback should an end user click through the link. Without wishing to play down the impact of phishing, business email compromise and its variants, the issue here is that we can either desensitise the end users so they stop listening or, worse, they think that this is the only threat they have to be aware of – and so create other areas of weakness to be exploited.

Awareness programmes may not suffer from the same limitations as a CBT or online course. A good instructor and compelling slides, backed with real-world stories, can be impactful and draw the audience in. Unfortunately, the time and cost of preparing such a programme, allied to the time and cost of actually getting it in front of the business, militate against such programmes being run frequently if at all.

Use of intranet or a security website

Another frequently used delivery method is the intranet and the 'security website'. The idea behind these is quite simple – a place where anyone can find what they need to know about security. The website can contain policies, CBT, presentations and can act as another awareness tool. Like any website, the security website needs frequent attention to keep it up to date, fresh and interesting. The maintenance of such a website takes time; writing or finding articles and content takes further time and effort. Unfortunately, the time needed for website maintenance can be gradually taken away by more important tasks, so the website loses its freshness and starts to become out of date. There is then of course a vicious cycle; it requires too much effort to update the website; no one visits the website, so why spend the effort on updating it; and so on. The website suffers from the same problem as 'merch'; it is passive and relies on people actively visiting it and looking for what they want.

Newsletters

Finally, there is the newsletter or weekly update email approach. Still used by many organisations, the corporate newsletter would seem to be an ideal vehicle for keeping security in people's minds. Similar to the website, effort is required to write the articles and hit the deadlines for publication. It is often difficult to know if the newsletter and individual articles are being read and to then measure the impact of any articles therein. Articles are much more effective when tied into other work – such as a phishing campaign – so each is reinforcing the other and readers get a sense of the wider picture. In some cases, different functions, regions or other corporate entities may produce their own newsletter – with perhaps a resulting negative impact on the overall readership of any of the newsletters received.

The mechanism or mechanisms by which we deliver our messages will impact the effectiveness of our campaigns. Different generations have learned to consume information in different ways and from different media, so we should look to use a blend of approaches to get our message across to the various audiences in an organisation. Using the same old approaches, for example email and print, may result in a percentage of our audience simply not seeing them – especially if our audience is on Slack (or similar) and Teams (or similar).

Now, this does not mean we should rush and create videos and images that would grace a TikTok, Instagram or YouTube account. Instead, think about how these and other media are used to get messages across to a wide audience. Clear messaging, supported by relevant visuals, in a time limited format lies at the heart of these approaches and result in an impactful and easy to understand package.

Despite the many routes we use to put our messages across, it can seem that nothing works; so, perhaps, it's not us, it's them?

PROBLEM EXISTS BETWEEN CHAIR AND KEYBOARD

We've all heard this or similar phrases about non-IT people; we may have used them ourselves. This simple phrase and accompanying attitude also sum up one of our biggest problems: we don't 'get' the very people to whom we are trying to communicate. You can argue that this phrase (and its kin) reflects our own culture, in that we believe outsiders to be either uninterested, unintelligent or unable to do the (simple) things we tell them.

Now, before I get accused of painting employees as being completely unconcerned about information security, let me add this very large caveat: most employees try their best every day. They try to remember the right way of doing things, follow the processes and procedures and do all the other things expected of them at work. Cybersecurity is just one more thing they have to remember and do.

Let's take a step back and think about our non-IT, non-cybersecurity colleagues. Typically, they're employed to do a job in which IT plays a subordinate and supporting role. They're expected to know how to use IT at some level; and the expectation is they know how to use email, word processing, spreadsheet and presentation software. Little or no training will be given when they join the organisation and it is likely that any training funds they receive will go towards their professional development. We talk of people and staff becoming computer and technology literate, but that isn't necessarily true; they are much better at using technology, because it has been simplified – think of app stores, automatic updates and so on. Again, I am not doing down our non-IT colleagues; rather I am challenging our assumptions about what they really know when it comes to IT and what we really expect of them. If, for example, a user is used to going to an app store, downloading the app they want with minimal effort and then using it, then can we really expect them to know how to change the configuration or profile in a business app?

We should reflect on the messages we send as well; all too often we exhort people 'not to click on links or attachments' or 'don't click on links or attachments you don't trust' in emails but then we send people emails with links in – and ask them to click on them! Put yourselves in the shoes of someone who receives these messages; first, it's incredibly confusing as I am being told one thing and then asked to do another. Second, I'm being told to make judgement calls in the work environment that I may not have the context, decision framework or understanding to make. In some cases, telling people to do certain things such as 'hover over the link' and see what the Uniform Resource Locator (URL) is can be worse than no advice at all – how does a non-specialist know the URL is a compromise tool? Finally, I am being told it's OK to click on certain links or attachments as they come from someone in the organisation with a particular role; but I don't know that person, nor do I understand where they fit in with my role or my sphere of interest. Without delving too much into the mechanics of trust, why should anyone trust you as the cybersecurity person? Why should they follow your advice when you seem to be contradicting it? As a result, what we think is a clear and unambiguous message is in fact the opposite and, if anything, sows doubt about us, our knowledge and why we should be believed.

We could argue that the problem does exist between chair and keyboard; but perhaps it is our chair and keyboard, not those of the non-IT specialist. In any business, like-minded individuals group together and develop their own culture, and their own assumptions and language. These groups can become closed shops, where the group opinions are perceived as being truth, not just opinion, and then start to be reflected back within the group, gaining veracity with each repetition.[39] The peril of groupthink[40] can also occur, so that decisions are made using the same terms of reference and with a desire not to destroy or upset the group. As a result, we believe what we (and our group) believe, and we believe that what we communicate to everyone outside the group is rational, clear and understandable because our group agree that is the case.

FOCUSING ON OURSELVES ALONE

Cybersecurity is not necessarily the best-loved part of an organisation, nor the best-financed. As a result, the team, function or individuals can become very closed and adopt an 'us against the world' mentality. It's not unusual: many other functions in a business do it as well.

Unfortunately, this can mean that cybersecurity professionals stop looking for new ideas and for help in performing tasks outside the normal range of activities. When thinking about awareness, training and education, we'll probably find that a significant percentage of cybersecurity professionals have never received formal training in how to create, populate and run cybersecurity programmes, how to measure their impact or how to measure the quality of the content. For example, security awareness occupies two pages in the *CISSP Official Study Guide* (Stewart et al., 2015) and these pages are concerned more with the setting up and management of the programmes, than the actual delivery. It's probably also true that very few cybersecurity professionals have been exposed to pedagogical thinking, the theories about learning styles and marketing and communication methods. Again, this is not to downplay the knowledge and skills of the cybersecurity professional, but the items mentioned in the previous sentence are usually outside the knowledge required of such a professional, and the demands of the role do not allow time for learning this knowledge.

As a result, when designing or looking at awareness campaigns, the same 'tried and tested' methods are adopted; new ideas are either not known about or not applied as there isn't time to learn, test and then apply them. This problem isn't new; for example, Thomson and von Solms published a paper in 1998 in which they stated:

> Techniques borrowed from the field of social psychology, which have been largely ignored in current awareness programs, are highlighted in order to show how they could be utilized to improve the effectiveness of the awareness program.

Much research, both academic and business, has focused on how to integrate non-security thinking, techniques and approaches with awareness. For example, using marketing techniques and treating non-security staff as customers has frequently been discussed; attempts to use gamification schemes described; and tactics such as influencing and drip-feeding information to arouse and maintain interest. However, much of this hasn't yet borne fruit in organisations, mainly because of inertia, time and cost pressures and the 'ourselves alone' mentality described at the beginning of this section.

Overcoming this issue of 'ourselves alone' is hard. One of the most pertinent and interesting insights about security awareness is given by the Information Security Forum (2020) in their *Standard of Good Practice*. Paraphrasing somewhat, the relevant section states inter alia,

> ... cybersecurity awareness programmes designed and delivered by dedicated, specialist learning and development professionals *and other subject matter experts (such as internal communications and marketing)* (emphasis added).

That widely accepted statements of good practice still need to explicitly tell us to work with other people highlights how rare such cross-disciplinary efforts are, even in 2020. It is a truism that good people seek out people who can complement them; if you are strong in finance but weak in marketing, you work with someone with the reverse skill mix. We should do the same and actively seek out other experts' opinions, advice and help – 'ourselves together' if you like – to seek new ways of telling our stories and new tools to communicate our message.

AWARENESS, BEHAVIOUR AND CULTURE

All the authors of this book agree that 'the objectives of a cybersecurity awareness campaign should always be to change behaviour for the better and to strengthen cybersecurity culture'.[41]

For us, awareness is not the be all and end all. It is in fact one of three factors that can be used in combination to improve cybersecurity in an organisation. It is often a stated desire that we, as cybersecurity professionals, want to change the culture and create a 'security culture' in our organisations. Awareness is not enough on its own and we need to harness other tools and techniques to transform awareness into a tool to change behaviour and strengthen culture.

Behaviour change is not easy – ask anyone who has tried to stop smoking or keep to a diet or exercise regime – but there is a wealth of published material and expertise covering this topic. One of the more popular approaches was 'Nudge Theory', as put forward in *Nudge: Improving Decisions about Health, Wealth and Happiness* (Thaler and Sunstein, 2009). Simply put, a nudge makes it more likely that an individual will make a particular choice, or behave in a particular way, by altering the environment so that automatic cognitive processes are triggered to favour the desired outcome. Examples include placing fruit at eye level (or by the tills) in shops and chocolate lower down;[42] making green energy deals the default; and placing hand sanitiser dispensers in easy to reach places in hospital wards to encourage hand hygiene for visitors and staff.[43]

We deliberately set our vision wider than the individual and their struggle to change behaviour. It is well known that a host of factors influence behavioural change. In the organisational context, which is what we are most interested in, one of the key factors is organisational culture. We'll discuss what this term really means later in the book, but for the moment we'll adopt the simple definition of 'the ways we do things round here'. Importantly, we need to align our expected security behaviours with the normal behaviours expected and set by the organisational culture. Simply telling people to do something that goes against the culture is doomed to failure. Instead, awareness and behaviour must work within and with the culture to accomplish lasting change and improvements in cybersecurity.

This book, based on our experience, makes the explicit link that awareness is there to change behaviour. We can make people aware that it is better to eat fruit than chocolate (or other junk food) – but if we change something that helps people to turn awareness into (easy) action, then awareness is turned into concrete actions or thought. For us as security professionals, behaviour is a key part of our defences. Think of all the times we exhort people 'not to click on links', 'don't open emails from people you don't know' or 'don't leave your computer unlocked'; in fact, all of these are learned behaviours. We are (subconsciously) asking people to change behaviour but not following it up with the insights needed to make that behaviour change or stick.

We will look further into behaviour and behaviour change in this book and how we can use well-known techniques to encourage simple actions that make a big difference to our security. Behaviour change is not an overnight phenomenon and there can be many setbacks and false starts. However, as we discuss, using the twin tools of awareness and behaviour change can increase the probability that change will happen and, most importantly, become the new norm (or the change will 'stick').

Recalling our previous discussion, we identified six factors that can make up a culture. I'd like to draw your attention to three components of the cultural web: stories and myths, rituals and routines, and control systems. Stories are an incredibly powerful way of transmitting shared or expected values and behaviours and what happens to those who adopt or reject those values or behaviours. Rituals and routines also create and impress expected values and behaviours on new and existing staff. Control systems also impress and reward expected behaviour, making behaviour even more significant. If people are rewarded (in whatever way) for following expected behaviour, then they will copy the expected behaviour.

We can quickly see that culture has a significant behavioural component. Change the behaviours, change the stories, rituals and rewards and you can change the culture. We talk of creating or maintaining a 'security culture' in our organisation and how awareness can help us in that task. With such a dependence on behaviour, we can quickly see that awareness on its own will have little impact. We thus go back to the comment at the beginning of this section, 'change behaviour for the better and strengthen cybersecurity culture'. One of our levers to change culture is behaviour.

In a manner similar to behaviour change, culture change is not an overnight phenomenon. We can address the creation and maintenance of a 'security culture' through small, meaningful behaviour changes. Trying to change a culture through a single massive intervention is risky – and just because chief executive officers (CEOs) have managed it in the past, doesn't mean it is a blueprint for the future.[44] It is often easier to change culture through small, well-defined changes and use these as stepping stones or employ their combined effect to make the required changes. Importantly, to change culture, we need to understand and define what the culture already is – a task we will examine later in the book.

So, to finish this introduction, let me provide you with a simple model of the ABCs (Figure 1.2).

From this diagram, I hope you can see that the three components of the model are (intimately) linked and that a change in one will affect the others for good or bad. The 'ABC wheel' also exhorts you to think how to use the components to best effect, so if you want to change behaviour, you examine how both awareness and culture can positively contribute.

SUMMARY

Cybersecurity awareness is important. Organisations are becoming ever more reliant on technology and data and this reliance is set to increase, as more and more data is generated by people and machines. As this reliance and dependence increases, so

Figure 1.2 Simple cybersecurity ABC model

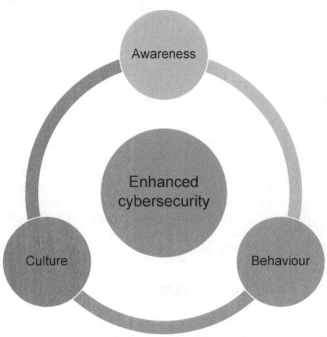

the effects of an incident also rise – not just in terms of time lost in managing the incident but in terms of regulatory and legal fines, brand and reputation damage, and external scrutiny. The cost of an awareness programme is certainly less than the cost of a breach.

However, despite its importance, getting security awareness to work is a perennial issue. This chapter has discussed some of the reasons behind why we struggle to make awareness work. We believe that awareness can only work if it is part of something larger and used in conjunction with the tools and techniques to change behaviour and strengthen culture from a security perspective. The next chapters will examine the ABCs – awareness, behaviour and culture – in much more detail and provide a new approach to delivering the lasting change and culture for which we all strive.

2 UNDERSTANDING CYBERSECURITY AWARENESS

Jessica Barker

In this chapter, we are going to explore why cybersecurity awareness matters at the organisational level, what we mean by cybersecurity awareness and how awareness of cybersecurity has, in general, evolved over the last few decades. We will elevate this discussion so that we are not addressing awareness in isolation, but rather so that we start to address awareness in terms of its relationship with behaviour and culture – a theme that will continue throughout the rest of the book. Finally, we will address the importance of attaching metrics to awareness-raising initiatives and how to make the most of your organisational resources.

WHY WE NEED CYBERSECURITY AWARENESS

When people think of 'insiders' within the context of cybersecurity, most automatically think of malicious insiders. Malicious insiders are very newsworthy when it comes to breaches; disgruntled employees (or former employees) taking revenge over a (perceived) wrongdoing always grab headlines, for example. When a malicious insider strikes, they often know which information to steal, where to get the most information, potentially how to take it without being identified and what to do with it to cause the most harm or reap the greatest benefit from it. This makes malicious insiders costly for organisations. However, they are not so numerous. It is far more common for an organisation to have a breach as the result of non-malicious action, by people simply making mistakes, than it is from malicious insiders. The Verizon Data Breach Investigations Report 2020, analysing 157,525 incidents and 3,950 data breaches, reported that 'errors' were the causal events in 22 per cent of breaches, 22 per cent involved phishing and 37 per cent of breaches involved either the theft of credentials or used credentials that had already been stolen (Verizon, 2020).

Cybercriminals manipulating unwitting people or taking advantage of human error is generally the biggest issue for organisations, and this is why awareness is so important. In 2020, ClubCISO surveyed 100 chief information security officers (CISOs) about the cause of any material cybersecurity incidents in their organisations over the previous 12 months, as part of an annual information security maturity report. According to the results, 14 per cent of respondents said malicious insider activity was the cause of a material incident, 42 per cent reported non-malicious insider activity as a cause and 40 per cent selected malicious outsider or cybercriminal activity (ClubCISO, 2020). These latter two statistics likely go hand-in-hand, with malicious outsiders taking advantage of non-malicious insiders, for example through spear-phishing emails or poorly configured systems in which access has been accidentally left open. This highlights the importance of awareness, with non-malicious insider activity three times as likely to be identified as the cause of an incident than malicious insider activity. Indeed, we can take this a step further and argue that awareness is important for mitigating malicious insider, as well as non-malicious insider, activity: the more people are aware of cybersecurity, the more malicious activity is likely to stand out and be identified.

These statistics highlight why we need awareness in cybersecurity: while the term may sound like a very technical one, much of cybersecurity involves people. Whether at the corporate or personal level, we cannot force people to behave securely online, but they, and we, may suffer if they do not. In this way, cybersecurity is much like public health. We cannot force people to be vaccinated, regularly wash their hands, cover their mouths and noses when they sneeze or engage in the other day-to-day activities that help prevent the spread of diseases. But, if people do not engage in those activities, they are more likely to catch and spread infectious diseases. For the better protection of individuals, organisations and countries, we need to effectively raise awareness of cybersecurity across the board. This involves understanding what has an impact, to such an extent that people don't merely listen to what we have to say but are influenced by our communications, to the degree that they are intrinsically motivated to act in security-positive ways.

Awareness can be understood in many different ways and has long been the subject of analysis in the social sciences. Many initiatives in society seek our awareness, from public health campaigns to advertisements, and organisations often need employees to be aware of various issues too. The success of awareness-raising initiatives varies wildly. In this chapter and the next, we will look at what we can do to raise awareness of cybersecurity (the 'A' of the cybersecurity ABCs) in a manner that has a positive impact on behaviours and cultures.

INTRODUCTION TO CYBERSECURITY AWARENESS

How do we define 'cybersecurity awareness'? Is it awareness of the threats? Or awareness of the best practices to follow to be more secure online?

In the previous chapter, we looked at the NIST definition of awareness, taken from the Special Publication 800-16, which describes awareness as something largely passive, that is intended to focus individuals' attention on IT security concerns so that they can respond accordingly.

If we look to 'cybersecurity', the *Oxford English Dictionary* describes this as: 'The state of being protected against the criminal or unauthorised use of electronic data, or the measures taken to achieve this.'

Therefore, we can understand 'cybersecurity awareness' to be: focusing individuals' attention on protecting against the criminal or unauthorised use of electronic data, so that they can respond accordingly.

When raising awareness of cybersecurity, I have seen many organisations focus solely on the threats. Of course, we must address the threats when we communicate about cybersecurity but taking a narrow view on this can limit the success of your awareness-raising programme.

For example, over the last few years, I have seen many organisations focus wholly on raising awareness of phishing attacks via email. This is a threat that individuals need to be aware of, with social engineering representing a huge issue for many organisations, but a holistic approach to awareness-raising, which includes phishing, will be more effective in long-term awareness, behaviour and cultural change than narrow campaigns like this. When I ask end users how they define cybersecurity, those in organisations that have focused on phishing at the cost of wider awareness-raising will often give very limited answers, with a perception of cybersecurity that stops at malicious links and attachments in emails. Meanwhile, social engineering attacks are increasingly utilising phone calls (often called vishing), messaging applications and social media platforms. If we focus simply on social engineering via emails, for example, then we leave people more exposed to attacks when cybercriminals evolve their methods.

The threats from cyber insecurity are evolving, and change frequently, with new threats sometimes emerging on a daily basis. Effective cybersecurity awareness-raising switches people's mindsets on to security in general, rather than raising their awareness merely with regard to a few current threats.

Awareness of cybersecurity has transformed in recent years. In the late 1990s and early 2000s, there was a trend of films specifically about hacking, including *Hackers*, *The Net*, *Swordfish* and *The Matrix* series. From 2010 onwards, more films have incorporated cybersecurity as an element in the plot, an integral and interwoven part of the narrative, such as *The Girl with the Dragon Tattoo* series, *James Bond: Skyfall* and *Fast and Furious 8*. This parallels the mainstreaming of cybersecurity more generally, with a recognition that internet technology is now an established part of our lives and security issues come part and parcel with that. Cybersecurity is also a prominent topic in the news, with regular reporting of data breaches and cyberattacks hitting the headlines. This has generated more awareness of the field in general. Cybersecurity is now a household topic of conversation (although understanding and engagement are still lacking).

To start thinking deeply about cybersecurity awareness, it can be helpful to first consider the concept of situational awareness. Situational awareness can be understood, essentially, as the ability to know what is happening around you. It is a concept that will be familiar to pilots, who must maintain a constant awareness of the operation of the airplane they are flying at the same time as remaining aware of changing environmental factors. In terms of cybersecurity, we want people to be aware of what is happening around them while they handle information and engage with technology, whether this is opening emails, using social media or discussing work with a colleague while on the train.

The growth in reporting of cyberattacks and data breaches has also led to more emphasis on awareness at the company level. Board members read about cybersecurity threats and attacks in newspapers and question their security and IT staff about how their company fares in relation to the news stories they have digested. Many of my clients have had their board actively request more cybersecurity awareness-raising and bring questions to their CISO based on articles they have read in the press.

I recently delivered a session to the board of a global law firm, including live demonstrations of password cracking and a spear-phishing attack, in which the majority of the executives stayed for half an hour longer than the scheduled session, making themselves late for their next meetings, to ask questions and seek further advice. Even just a few years ago, this kind of engagement was very hard to find.

SENIOR-LEVEL BUY-IN AND ENGAGEMENT

Senior-level engagement is a highly influential factor in the success of an awareness-raising campaign. When people work in an organisation, they often look to how their bosses are behaving to determine what is expected and acceptable, and what is not, in their own behaviour. Social proof is the phenomenon of people modelling their behaviour based on how they see others behave, and when it comes to social proof, people we respect, or who are in a position of authority, are more influential on our behaviour (Cialdini, 2007). This has parallels with social learning theory, which describes the way in which new patterns of behaviour are acquired by observing the behaviour of others (Bandura, 1971). In the (ISC)[2] Awareness, Behaviour and Culture Workshops (ABC Workshops) of 2017, participants (who were cybersecurity professionals from different organisations) described senior executives in their organisations jumping over security barriers because they had forgotten their access badges, saving passwords to Excel files and asking for company information to be emailed to their personal email accounts. This frustrated participants, who recognised that when their senior leadership show disregard towards the cybersecurity policies it undermines their efforts to effectively raise awareness, change behaviours and positively influence cybersecurity culture.

Senior executives are also an attractive target for cybercriminals. They have access to a lot of information and money, and they have authority and influence that can be exploited in social engineering attacks. They also often have high personal net worth, and so can be a target for many different reasons. Given these factors, and the power of social proof and social learning, effectively engaging with the senior level of an organisation is fundamental to cybersecurity awareness and behaviours in an organisation as a whole.

To engage with senior executives, follow the same approach as with any other audience: make it relevant to them and speak their language. Technical jargon will not cut it here; speaking in business terms will have much greater impact. So, rather than focusing on vulnerabilities, focus on the impact of the vulnerabilities in terms of the particular organisation. Wherever possible, put this in financial terms. Use case studies from your own organisation, or from organisations in the same sector. Make it clear that cybersecurity is not just a technical subject that the IT team can 'fix' – for example, if there is a data breach, will it be the IT team who write the press release? Of course not; it will be the public relations (PR) and communications experts. This is just one example that highlights that cybersecurity is not simply an IT issue. Talk about solutions, what defences are currently working and where you need action and investment.

AWARENESS ALONE IS NOT THE ANSWER

We are at a stage where awareness of cybersecurity has indeed never been higher. In the ABC Workshops we conducted over four conferences in 2017, we surveyed 118 information security professionals drawn from the participants: of these, only 5 per cent were from organisations that carried out no cybersecurity awareness-raising activities. Most organisations, regardless of size or sector, will now undertake some form of activities to raise awareness of cybersecurity among their workforce.

However, this is not to say that understanding of cybersecurity is high or that behaviours and cultures have been transformed. Awareness alone does not necessarily change behaviours: if it did, fast food restaurants would have gone out of business a long time ago. It is possible to be aware of something but to behave in a way which is at odds with that awareness. With this in mind, the objectives of a cybersecurity awareness campaign should always be to change behaviour for the better and to strengthen cybersecurity culture. To achieve this, we need to consider how we raise awareness in a deeper, more meaningful and more engaging way.

> When I begin planning an awareness-raising campaign with a client, I always start with culture. What kind of cybersecurity (and wider) culture do you have in the organisation and what kind of cybersecurity culture do you want? Then, I move back a level. What kind of behaviours would reflect that culture? Once those have been identified, we have an idea of the outcomes we are aiming for with the awareness-raising campaign: we want to see the identified behaviours as a result of a shift in understanding about cybersecurity.

If we want awareness-raising to be deeply effective, then we want it to engage in shifting the understanding about cybersecurity to such an extent that it positively influences behavioural change. To achieve this, I have identified core questions that we can consider when planning an awareness campaign. We not only need to start with why, but we need to end with it, too, to inspire people to engage in the messages we are spreading (Sinek, 2011). In this way, it fits perfectly with the NIST definition of awareness, by focusing individuals' attention on IT security concerns so that they can respond accordingly. For awareness-raising to be most impactful, it should answer the following questions:

- Why is cybersecurity relevant to the people you are communicating with?
- How does cybercrime actually operate?
- What can people do to better-protect themselves?
- Why will the behaviours that you are recommending work?

In considering these, we need to answer the inevitable question: Why would cybercriminals want my data? There are two levels to this. First, why the individuals may be targeted. People often lose sight of the value of the information that they are handling, or fail to consider that the small company they work for may be targeted as a route to their big clients, or simply do not understand that their access to the network could provide a pivot point for criminals to move throughout the rest of the system. Second, there is also often a lack of awareness regarding the non-targeted nature of many cyberattacks (for example, evidence suggests that the UK National Health Service (NHS) was not targeted with the WannaCry attack in May 2017, but being a victim of the attack cost the NHS £92 million and over 19,000 patient appointments had to be cancelled as a result of it; Cyber Security Policy, 2018).

The intangible nature of cyber insecurity is one of the key challenges we face when raising awareness. Cybercrime is not something that most people see and feel until it happens to them. Even then, many individuals and organisations can be a victim of cybercrime for a long time before they discover it, if they discover it at all. Beyond this, many people work with computers, but don't necessarily **understand** computers. This means they may find it hard to intuitively understand how something as seemingly innocuous as clicking links or reusing passwords could be so fundamental in enabling cybercrime.

We have also made cybersecurity burdensome for end users. Telling people not to click links? That is a core part of using the internet and, for many, fundamental to their ability to do their job. Advising people to use a different, complicated, random and long password for each of their accounts? When many people have more than 20 or 30 accounts (perhaps even more than 100), this becomes impossible without writing them down, storing them in an electronic file or using a password manager. Yet many cybersecurity professionals remain unwilling to consider that writing passwords down may be the best solution for many home internet users. Understanding of password managers is also very low: many people are not aware of what they are or why they would be less risky than reusing weak passwords across all of their accounts. It is the same with two-factor authentication (2FA): in a survey of 1,000 people in the UK, which I conducted in 2019, 62 per cent of people did not know what 2FA is and only 26 per cent of people were using it.[45]

Having delivered awareness-raising sessions to tens of thousands of people in the last two years alone, I have found that live demonstrations of cyber insecurity are one of the most engaging and effective awareness-raising activities possible. When people witness password cracking, for example, they understand the importance of strong and unique passwords in a way that no theoretical explanation can match. The danger of live demonstrations of cyber insecurity is that they are scary. In the following chapter, I discuss the psychology of fear and the importance of carefully handling fear-based responses to your awareness-raising activities. The key to this, and to awareness-raising activities in general, is empowerment. It is imperative that we communicate in simple terms what people can do to better protect themselves from the threats we have been demonstrating. Central to this is providing the tools that people need to engage in the behaviours we recommend. For example, if you raise awareness of spear-phishing emails, it is important to communicate what people should do if they receive a suspected phishing email or if they are worried about a link they've clicked on or an attachment they have downloaded (a good 'report a phish' process is fantastic, for example with a 'report a phish' button in email clients). If you've delivered a password-cracking demonstration, simply telling people that they need to use unique, random and complicated passwords for each of their accounts will not suffice. How will they do that? Does the organisation provide them with a password manager, and will there be workshops and simple, concise guidance to get people up-and-running?

Cybersecurity awareness-raising can too often focus on problems, when we need to emphasise solutions. We must not forget that NIST defines awareness as focusing individuals' attention on IT security concerns **so that they can respond accordingly** (emphasis author's own).

UTILISING METRICS

Working on the human side of cybersecurity, one of the most common questions I hear is 'how can you measure any of this?' We are an industry that likes data, and I often encounter the perception that technical defences can be measured but human defences cannot. This is far from the case. Any measurements in cybersecurity are far from 100 per cent reliable as we are inherently dealing with 'unknown unknowns'. We make the best of the data that we have when it comes to everything from the number of attacks, attribution of attacks, cost of incidents and ability of technical controls to mitigate the risks. The same should be true of awareness, behaviour and culture; let's consider what data we can get and let's make the most of it.

There are many solutions to facilitate the setting and monitoring of metrics in cybersecurity.

> At Cygenta, the company I co-founded, the approach we take is to consider key areas of culture, analyse how individuals perform in relation to those key areas and see how this changes according to training and other communications.

It is imperative not to approach the setting of metrics as an avenue to attribute blame to the individuals (gross misconduct, malicious behaviour and neglect aside, of course). Instead, see this as a way of understanding what works, and what doesn't, when it comes to your awareness-raising initiatives. Identify the behaviours that you want to see change, measure those behaviours, conduct an awareness-raising activity, then measure again. Repeat this approach and before too long you will have a good data set with regard to your awareness-raising endeavours. This should be extremely helpful in identifying what works (and what does not) and may also provide useful metrics to be reported to senior executives, for example if you are seeking more investment to boost the awareness-raising budget.

MAKING THE MOST OF YOUR RESOURCES

When it comes to awareness-raising, we often have to make the most of what we have. It is common for resources to be restricted in one way or another, so how can we make the most of our resources?

Budget

Budget is a frequent challenge in cybersecurity overall, and often in human-based approaches in particular, which is why metrics are so valuable. When you can prove that your awareness-raising activities are having a positive impact on mitigating risks, you are in a much stronger position to defend or increase your budget.

If you're in a small organisation, you don't have to spend a great deal of money on awareness-raising to have a big impact. Make cybersecurity a standing item on the agenda at team meetings and discuss a cybersecurity story that has hit the headlines by explaining what has happened, what the impact was and how it could relate to your organisation. If you're in a large organisation, work with your colleagues across the business to identify any campaigns where your messaging is aligned with theirs. For example, some organisations run sessions on digital wellbeing as part of wider wellbeing and health weeks, and that way they can bring cybersecurity awareness-raising to the fore in other campaigns.

Computer-based training

I am frequently asked how organisations that lack resources (time and people, as well as money) can improve their awareness-raising training. A lot of organisations attempt to solve this problem with computer-based training packages. However, these solutions are not all created equal. Many have not been designed with a people-centric approach and so fail to tackle the important questions I listed above (the whys, hows and whats) and therefore inevitably fail to engage or challenge people. When this is the case, they become a 'click-through' and forgettable experience that will have no positive impact on cybersecurity behaviour or culture. Poorly designed computer-based training will most likely make your job harder, adding to the perception that cybersecurity is dry, onerous and something to be avoided or dismissed as quickly as possible.

When designed with people in mind, computer-based training can be a great addition to your toolset, enabling you to reinforce and scale your efforts. The training should be digestible, engaging, fun, informative and people should be tested (truly tested, not a test they can easily brute force, for example, with tests that always include the same questions and answers, so people can simply retake the test until they pass it), making use of multi-media elements as much as possible.

Cybersecurity champions

A cybersecurity champion or ambassador programme is another way of scaling up awareness-raising activities in organisations. A champion programme follows a similar approach to health and safety in many organisations. People who are not experts or specialists are recruited to represent cybersecurity in their team or department. I have seen this approach reap many benefits, with champions facilitating better two-way conversations between the business and the security team, greater reporting of incidents and a more effective flow of awareness-raising communications. When managed well, and in the right culture, a champions programme can amplify your messages and extend their reach.

However, there are some general points to take into account when considering whether a champions programme would work for you and your organisation.

First, who will be the champions and how will you recruit them? It is usually an unpaid, volunteer position and is best not implemented as a 'police force'. The organisations that I have seen successfully implement a champions programme have recruited people who have asked frequent questions of the security team, reported incidents, enquired about security at home as well as at work, or expressed an interest in transitioning their career to security one day.

Champions need to be kept engaged, so it is worthwhile considering how you will keep them motivated. Some great mechanisms for this are extra training, emails to their line managers highlighting their contribution to the programme, support for better security at home and, of course, goodies, which are often well-received. Some champions programmes use a mascot, selected by the champions themselves, and featured on mugs, T-shirts and stickers that are given to the champions.

No amount of goodies will make up for a lack of support, however, and so this is one of the most important considerations. While you would not expect the champions to be experts, and this is not the idea behind the concept, they will most likely want to be equipped with a decent general level of understanding about cybersecurity. How will you provide them with some training and communications? For example, you could consider whether it is feasible to occasionally bring in an external speaker on cybersecurity to run a session for the champions, or explore whether they can have a day a year at a local cybersecurity conference. These are a couple of ideas that should keep your champions engaged and fulfil some training requirements. However, you will likely still receive questions from them, either directly or which they have received from their colleagues: how will you manage those?

If possible, it is a good idea to have a forum, say on your intranet, or group in an instant messaging service (for example, if your organisation uses Slack or Teams) where the champions can communicate with one another, asking and answering questions among themselves. This is an empowering approach that also offers the opportunity to reduce the burden on you.

A champions network may enable you to scale up your awareness programme, but it does still place demands on your time, with regard to training and supporting the champions themselves. It is worth acknowledging this up-front and being realistic about the amount of time you have available, whether you can rely on other team members to support you in delivering the champions programme or if there are self-sustaining mechanisms you can put in place, such as the forum example above.

SUMMARY

In this chapter, we have looked at why cybersecurity awareness matters, how we can define and understand awareness and how it has grown over the last few decades. We have also started to address how awareness fits with behaviour and culture, which will be an ongoing theme of this book. We have looked at how to make your awareness-raising initiatives more impactful, for example with an effective champions programme. In the next chapter, we will look at other ways to build awareness and how to do this without evoking negative psychological responses to discussing a subject that arouses fear.

NEXT STEPS

Let's look at some next steps for you to review in terms of awareness-raising in your organisation:

- Do you perceive cybersecurity awareness-raising in your organisation to be focused on a few narrow threats or to take more of a situational-awareness approach?

- Consider how the senior executives in your organisation engage in cybersecurity and whether they contribute to cybersecurity awareness in a positive way:
  - Have they made an official statement about the importance of cybersecurity, for example in a video that can be used as part of awareness-raising?
  - Do they visibly practice positive (or negative) cybersecurity behaviours in a way that supports (or undermines) social proof and social learning of cybersecurity good practices?

- Has your organisation defined what cybersecurity culture it is seeking to develop and what behaviours would demonstrate that culture? Is awareness-raising linked to these goals?

- Review some of the awareness materials in your organisation and consider whether they communicate why this issue is so important, not simply what to do or what not to do.

- What metrics do you have in place to track the effectiveness of awareness-raising activities and how do these relate to behaviours and culture?

- Do you have a champions programme in place?
  - If you do, what stage is the programme at and what obstacles is it facing?
  - If you don't, what would it take to set one up? How can you use ideas from this chapter to identify, recruit and retain champions?

3   BUILDING CYBERSECURITY AWARENESS

Jessica Barker

In this chapter, we will explore cybersecurity awareness-raising in more detail, particularly focusing on techniques to raise awareness in a positive and effective way. This chapter will therefore introduce you to some ideas to implement in your organisation. We will also address the issue of fear, uncertainty and doubt (FUD). Unfortunately, the cybersecurity industry has relied on FUD to try to communicate cybersecurity messages for too long, often in an ineffective way. The way many use FUD can even backfire, leading to greater resistance to awareness messages, rather than greater engagement. There are many other ways we can talk about cybersecurity, and more positive ways. However, we must also recognise that raising awareness of cybersecurity does often inevitably mean discussing the threat, which can mean that the people we are communicating with feel fear. With this in mind, this chapter explores how we can talk about something scary in the most constructive, positive way.

Before we move on, however, we should tackle a fundamental question underpinning all of this: Is awareness-raising, in and of itself, always a good thing? Over the last few years, I have watched the cybersecurity industry change. In 2011, when I was beginning my career, I would often have to explain to people within the industry what I actually meant by 'the human side' of cybersecurity, and what it was that I actually did. That is no longer the case, as the human side of cybersecurity has massively grown in prominence.

With the growth in prominence of the human side of cybersecurity, there has been an associated sweeping narrative that 'people are the weakest link'. This is an unhelpful and, frankly, lazy narrative that some of us within the industry have fought hard to challenge, attempting to demonstrate that people can be the strongest link if given the correct support, awareness-raising and tools. The UK's National Cyber Security Centre (NCSC) has joined this call, with an ethos from its inception that promotes a positive and people-centric approach to security.[46]

With the rise in acceptance of people as an important factor in cybersecurity, there has been a prevalent assumption that, to solve the 'people problem', an organisation should carry out awareness-raising activities. However, awareness-raising comes in many forms and all of those forms are not equal. When you raise awareness of an issue, you may elicit unintended consequences. It is important to understand what some of those unintended consequences may be, how to limit their chances of emerging, and how to effectively deal with them if they arise. We will explore this issue more, as this chapter progresses.

Awareness-raising that is engaging, effective and empowering – and is conducted as part of a wider strategy focused on behaviour and culture – is immensely valuable to an organisation. So, how can we raise awareness of cybersecurity in a way that is engaging, effective and empowering?

People are more likely to engage in recommended behaviour if they understand why. I have seen this first-hand during my career delivering cybersecurity awareness-raising sessions in organisations of all sectors around the world. Cybersecurity can seem intangible: without deep technical knowledge and understanding, people often simply do not understand, for example, the importance of having unique, long and strong passwords or how clicking a malicious link in an email can allow a cybercriminal to access their machine, including all of the data on it, their microphone and webcam.

In the words of Simon Sinek, we need to start an awareness programme with 'why?' (Sinek, 2011). Telling people to have good passwords, to be careful of what they click on and to set up two-factor authentication is a list of commands. Why should they simply follow what you tell them, especially if it gets in the way of their primary purpose online, whether that's getting on with their work or catching up on social media?

Telling people why something is important is one thing but showing them takes your awareness-raising to a whole other level. You can tell people to have unique and strong passwords for all of their online accounts, but that just sounds like an unnecessary burden unless you help people understand why it is so important. When people **see** a password-cracking demonstration, they understand that millions of dictionary words can be cracked in less than a second with pre-built tools that are freely available for anyone to use. In this way, individuals experience a cyberattack in a safe environment, optimising their learning without the pain of a real incident. As Meier (2000, p. 28) said:

> If you seek information, read words
> If you seek understanding, have experiences.

THE FEYNMAN TECHNIQUE

Cybersecurity is a complicated subject. Richard Feynman, the Nobel prize-winning physicist, is renowned for being able to make the most complicated of subjects more accessible. We can adapt what has become known as the Feynman technique for our cybersecurity awareness-raising initiatives. The Feynman technique[47] can be broken down as follows:

Step 1: In a notebook or on a blank piece of paper, write the name of the concept or subject you are studying.

Step 2: Imagine you are teaching the subject to a child. Underneath the title, write an explanation of the concept or subject, using only plain language (avoiding jargon where possible, and defining it simply where it cannot be avoided). This will highlight what you know and, most importantly, what you don't fully understand.

Step 3: Focus on the areas that you have identified you do not understand. Go back to the source material, reread and relearn. Repeat Step 2 until there are no gaps in your knowledge.

Step 4: Look over your notes and simplify any complicated language. If you are paraphrasing the source material anywhere, then reword it. Use straightforward analogies and stories where they are helpful in bringing the subject to life.

> I find the Feynman technique to be the best way of learning about new concepts myself. As someone who focuses on the human side of cybersecurity, I pride myself on having strong technical understanding of the subject and on being able to translate technical messages in the awareness-raising activities and communications I deliver to clients. As cybersecurity is a constantly evolving field, I therefore have to learn about new technologies, vulnerabilities and attacks on an extremely regular basis, and I have to fully understand them because I may be asked to explain any aspect of them during awareness-raising for a client or indeed in a media appearance.

I have adapted the Feynman technique for awareness-raising workshops with clients. Here's how I use it for learning in a group:

Step 1: Give everyone in the room a new notebook or some blank paper. Split the room into two and assign a different cybersecurity topic to both halves. As I explain in Chapter 2, topics you cover in awareness-raising should be defined by behaviours that you want to influence. Choose two of the topics that you have identified as things that you want to raise awareness of within the organisation or group; for example, I will often assign CEO fraud to one group and ransomware to the other, or it could be password managers to one group and two-factor authentication to the other.

Step 2: Allow the individuals in each group a set amount of time (this will vary depending on how long you have with the group, but 20–30 minutes is good) to learn about their subject, using internet access or resources you have provided. Advise them to write notes using only plain language (avoiding jargon where possible and defining it simply where it cannot be avoided). Tell them to pretend they are teaching it to a child. Go around the room and check how people are doing, giving them support and assistance, without doing it for them.

Step 3: Have people pair up with someone from the other group and take turns explaining their subject to one another. Again, they should use only simple language, defining any jargon and using stories, examples and analogies. In explaining their subject to their partner and trying to answer any questions their partner may have, individuals will identify what they understood and where they had gaps in knowledge or questions; ask them to note these down.

Step 4: Ideally, Steps 2 and 3 should be repeated until there are no gaps in anybody's knowledge, but in a workshop scenario that often is not practical so Step 4 will probably need to be modified depending on the group and the time you have with them. If time allows, repeat Step 2 to enable people to plug the identified holes in their knowledge. If there is not time for that, work out what is best for the situation; for example, you can have people read out their questions and answer them yourself or collate all of the questions from the group and circulate answers later.

The most important thing to remember about the Feynman technique is that people don't remember what they are taught as well as what they have learned and explained to somebody else. So, the subject that they revised and communicated to their workshop partner will be the subject that they understand in the most depth. Of course, at the same time, you are raising awareness of both of the subjects that you focus on in a meaningful and interactive way. There are lots of ways you can follow up on the workshop, too. You could capture key points from the individuals as they are sharing their learning and put these together in a handout that you send around the group after the session, to prompt their memory of the learning and reinforce key messages. You may find that a few people in the workshop are especially keen to build on their learning, so they may even want to help develop the handout or you may want to engage these individuals as security champions (as discussed in Chapter 2).

Part of the beauty of the modified Feynman technique that I outline above is that it is interactive. You are not standing in front of people as an expert and expecting them to listen to you communicate about cybersecurity. It is not 'death by PowerPoint', but rather it is empowering and engaging. This is always the aim for cybersecurity awareness-raising: to be as empowering and engaging as possible. You want as many people as possible to be truly engaged in learning about the subject, feeling confident with a subject that is too often presented in an intimidating and elite manner.

ACCELERATED LEARNING

The modified Feynman technique also sits nicely with another great approach to awareness-raising, and that is Accelerated Learning.

I first heard about Accelerated Learning at the SANS European Security Awareness Summit in London in 2016. I go to hundreds of conferences and the SANS summit is one of my absolute highlights of the year, because it is focused on my passion (the human side of cybersecurity), and I'm in a room full of people who share that passion.

In 2016 Martine van de Merwe gave a talk showing methods to appeal to different kinds of learners, to keep participation high and to improve training results.[48] Although the term 'accelerated learning' was new to me, I discovered that I had in fact been using the approach in awareness-raising for a long time, without knowing the technical term for it.

Accelerated Learning is rooted in what we know about how the brain works, about getting and keeping people's attention, about motivating people and about the ways in which different people learn. An important part of Accelerated Learning is creating an atmosphere in which people feel confident and comfortable. The language you use to speak to those participating in training is really important, as we know from decades of psychological research. When you expect people to perform poorly and to be the 'weakest link in cybersecurity', they will be less likely to engage in the positive behaviours you are asking of them (in psychology, this is known as the Golem effect; Babad et al., 1982). When you empower and enable people, when you develop their confidence and believe in them, they will be more likely to engage in the positive cybersecurity behaviours that you are seeking to engender (known as the Pygmalion effect; Babad et al., 1982).

Accelerated Learning also promotes the use of different methods to engage people in training, because different people learn in different ways. These include:

- somatic or doing; for example, a workshop in which you have participants design their own phishing campaign (invoking the theory that you have to think like an attacker to defend against an attacker);

- auditory or talking and hearing; for example, the modified Feynman technique I outline above fits nicely into this category;

- visual or observing; a hacking demonstration is great for accessing this learning style;

- intellectual or problem-solving; for example, with a table-top exercise that walks participants through a breach scenario and asks them to respond to the breach, overcome obstacles and strategise solutions.

It can be argued that learning is optimised when we combine all four methods because it is not simply the case that different people learn in different ways, but rather that we can all benefit from multiple styles of learning (Meier, 2000, p. 42). If you can integrate the different learning styles in your awareness campaigns, you will engage more people, more deeply: 'Effective awareness requires consistent communication through several channels' (Beyer et al., 2015, p. 6).

FEAR APPEALS

Many clients have approached me in the past and asked me to design or deliver awareness-raising in their organisation with the goal of 'scaring people into behaving'.

I can understand the frustration behind this request. To an individual with a great deal of cybersecurity knowledge (and, perhaps, little knowledge of fields such as psychology, sociology, neuroscience or behavioural economics), it is frustrating and bewildering to see people be careless with passwords, hold the door open for anyone who wants to walk into their office, leave their workstations unlocked while they go out for lunch or click on links just because an email prompts them to do so. From the perspective of the average chief information security officer or security manager, such behaviour must surely be because those people do not understand the threat. If they understood the threat was real, then surely they would comply with all of the security rules?

When you communicate information to people with the intent of scaring them into a certain behaviour, you are invoking what is known as a 'fear appeal'. We see fear appeals all of the time, from television adverts warning of the importance of not driving after you have been drinking alcohol, to graphic images of smoking-related diseases on cigarette packets. Fear appeals have been used for at least the last six decades in various ways in society and we can look to psychological research to understand why some work and some do not, and therefore how best to talk about a scary subject if you want to prompt behavioural change.

The Extended Parallel Process Model is an extremely helpful framework that was developed by Kim Witte, a Speech Communications Professor, and that outlines how people react when confronted with a fear appeal (Witte, 1992). People process fear appeals in a certain way, without really being aware of it. First, they will assess whether they believe that the threat is real. I believe awareness-raising has succeeded in convincing most people that, yes, the cybersecurity threat is real. So, next they will assess whether they are susceptible to it, as an individual. If we do manage to convince people that they are susceptible to the threat, they will then go on to assess the responses we are recommending: do they understand the responses? Do they believe that the responses will be effective in mitigating the threat? Only if they answer yes to those questions, will they then consider whether they are personally capable of engaging in the responses.

The Extended Parallel Process Model is based on Protection Motivation Theory (Rogers, 1975) and the work of Howard Leventhal, a psychology professor (Rogers, 1975). In 1965, Leventhal conducted a very influential study looking at the relationship between fear arousal and actions. In the study, participants were provided with a high or low fear-arousing message about tetanus and were advised to have a vaccination. Half of the participants were also provided with a map of the local area, highlighting the location of the hospital, and were prompted to plan their day in order to visit the hospital and have the injection. Results showed that those provided with the high fear messaging had more positive intentions to have the vaccination (compared to those who received the low fear messaging), but that these intentions did not translate into action (they intended to have the injection, but they did not follow through with actually having it). However, the study also found that those who were provided with the map and encouraged to plan when they would have the injection were far more likely to follow through with the behaviour: 30 per cent of those who received the action instructions got the vaccination, whereas in the group that did not receive the action instructions, only 3 per cent got the vaccination (Leventhal et al., 1965).

In terms of cybersecurity, fear appeals often take the form of pictures of 'hackers' in hoodies and balaclavas in front of a green screen of 1s and 0s accompanied by statistics of how many companies and individuals get hacked every year and the associated cost. People respond to such fear appeals with doubts such as:

- Do cybercriminals exist, does data have value, are cyberattacks and data breaches common?

- Why would cybercriminals want my data?

- Will having long, complicated and unique passwords really do anything to protect me?

- Will clicking on a link really do any harm?

- How am I supposed to remember all of these different passwords?

- How can I do my job without clicking links in emails and downloading documents?

- How can I challenge colleagues trying to enter the building without wearing their badges? Won't they think I'm rude?

- Why should I lock my workstation when I walk away from it? Surely I can trust my colleagues?[49]

If at any point in this awareness-raising process, we fail to convince our audience that cybercriminals exist, that they personally are susceptible to a data loss or compromise, that the mitigations we recommend do work **and** that they are able to engage in those mitigations, then we are likely to provoke a defensive response from them: they will revert to acceptance or avoidance. This can take the shape of 'the problem is so big and I am not capable of all of those defences, so why bother? If it's that bad then it's inevitable' and 'this threat is overblown, IT are just trying to get us to do what they want, why bother?' and 'I'm too busy for that, I can't remember all of those passwords, I'll worry about it another day.'

These defensive reactions of reluctance, avoidance and denial are completely normal and are to be expected when we clumsily wield fear as a tool for awareness-raising, with no awareness ourselves of the psychological implications of how we communicate such scary messages.

> Fear appeals should be used cautiously, since they may backfire if audiences do not believe they are able to effectively avert a threat.
>
> (Witte and Alen, 2000)

When people are scared about something but do not understand how they are susceptible to the threat or, most importantly, how they can engage in better protecting themselves, they will engage not with the true danger (cybercrime) but rather with the emotional response: the fear. This is why they avoid the reality of the situation or choose to believe that you are exaggerating the threat. So, we need to be very careful when we use fear appeals. As an industry, we must move away from simply trying to scare people into behaving more securely and we must communicate in a responsible way when talking about cyber threats to ensure that people engage with the actual danger rather than just the emotional response that is aroused from hearing about the threat.

Psychological research suggests that the weaker the efficacy message (the communication that the individual can engage in behaviours to minimise the threat), the greater the fear control response (the defensive mechanisms of avoidance or denial):

If fear appeals are disseminated without efficacy messages, or with a one-line recommendation, they run the risk of backfiring, since they may produce defensive responses in people with low-efficacy perceptions.

(Witte and Alen, 2000)

When discussing the cybersecurity threat, you are inevitably discussing something scary. In fact, it can be argued that just saying the word 'cyberspace' will cause fear in some listeners as it is a vague and unknown word (Bada et al., 2015). I believe that tackling fear, uncertainty and doubt is central to awareness-raising, which is why I delivered a keynote on the topic at the RSA conference in San Francisco in 2020. So, how can we talk about this scary subject in a way that prompts positive, rather than negative, behavioural change?

ENABLING SELF-EFFICACY

Let's refer back to the Extended Parallel Process Model and consider how we should focus our awareness-raising messages if we want to be effective.

Step 1: Show people that the threat is real and that they are susceptible to it, for example by using references to real-world attacks and anecdotes that relate to their industry sector and job role as closely as possible. For example, rather than using general statistics on cybercrime, use statistics from your own company and explain that many cyberattacks are not targeted but you can become a victim nevertheless (the NHS WannaCry case study I discussed in Chapter 2 is an example of this). Showing hacking demonstrations is extremely effective here, as it opens people's eyes to the reality of how cybercrime is actually carried out. For example, with a password cracking demonstration, you can highlight that attackers do not target individuals and try to manually guess their password, but rather use a script and tools to compromise passwords from breached lists.

When people understand that the threat is real and that they are susceptible to it, they will be scared, and this must be handled responsibly. Do not leave them in this state. Instead, it is very important that you implement Step 2.

Step 2: This is where we focus on self-efficacy. Let's say you are running an awareness-raising session on passwords and you have delivered a password-cracking demonstration. Now, you need to explain to people what they can do to mitigate the risks and ensure that they have the tools and techniques available to them and the understanding and confidence to use those tools and techniques. It is not good enough to simply recommend that people have a unique and complicated password for each of their accounts (which possibly still expire on a regular basis despite the latest NCSC and NIST guidance[50]) and that people cannot write them down but rather must simply remember them. This is not realistic. You can train people in using passphrases, but it is still asking a great deal of their cognitive load that they should have a unique passphrase for each account.

So, let's unpick step 2 a bit: what are you going to ask them to do? The security burden of passwords cannot continue to fall so heavily on people; we need to provide people with the tools to manage unique, complicated passwords or they will continue to reuse weak ones. If there is a corporate password manager, then show them it and give them a demonstration, too. After giving the password-cracking demonstration, run password management workshops where you work with people step by step to get them set up and running with the password manager. Provide well-designed, visually appealing handouts that explain, in concise and simple terms, how to set up and use a password manager, ideally with contact details included so people can get in touch if they need more support.

If you want positive behavioural change to result from your awareness-raising, then it is imperative that people understand the action and why it will better protect them, and that they have tools in place that they feel confident using. As Witte and Alen commented:

> ... strong fear appeals and high-efficacy messages produce the greatest behavior change, whereas strong fear appeals with low-efficacy messages produce the greatest levels of defensive responses.
>
> (Witte and Alen, 2000)

At Cygenta, we regularly run hacking demonstrations as part of the awareness-raising programmes that we deliver. When people see a live demonstration of a spear-phishing attack, showing the criminal and the victim sides and just what the criminal is able to do from the click of a malicious link, this is a strong fear appeal and it must be handled carefully. It is vital, at this point, to communicate the relevance of this to the people in the room and to provide a strong self-efficacy message.

As another example, it is not enough to say to the participants 'be wary of the links you click on in emails'. This advice does not empower or enable the participant in any way. They will leave either terrified of clicking on any links or believing that the situation is so hopeless, or so exaggerated, that they might as well just carry on regardless. It is so much more empowering and enabling to show them what to do if they receive an email that they suspect may be phishing. Hopefully, your organisation has a 'report a phish' button in emails or an email address that people can send suspected phishes on to. If so, this is what you want to show people after you have raised their awareness about phishing, because this is the crucial high-efficacy message that you need to produce the greatest behavioural change. This fits perfectly with the NIST definition of awareness that we have referred to in Chapters 1 and 2: focusing individuals' attention on IT security concerns so that they can respond accordingly.

This approach is backed up by research by Ruiter, which analysed six decades of research into fear appeals:

> ... the elements of fear appeals most likely to motivate risk reduction behaviors are: (a) strengthening self-efficacy (i.e., suggesting that the person can successfully perform the recommended protective actions); (b) promotion of response efficacy (i.e. suggesting that the recommended action will avoid the danger); (c) awareness of susceptibility (i.e., suggesting that the threat is personally relevant); and not, (d) messages suggesting in an emotional way that the threat is severe.
>
> (Ruiter, 2014)

Self-efficacy is an important concept in cybersecurity. It is a person's belief in their ability to succeed in a specific situation or accomplish a specific task. Raising self-efficacy in awareness-raising activities is important because it fights against another common pitfall of awareness-raising: security fatigue.

AVOIDING SECURITY FATIGUE

It is both a blessing and a curse that cybersecurity now has such a high profile. The very large number of cyberattacks, data breaches and vulnerabilities makes our profession such a challenging industry to work in. The fact that so many of these cyberattacks, data breaches and vulnerabilities are now public can be a good driver for engaging board members and colleagues in the subject: awareness of cybersecurity, in a very general sense, has never been higher. However, the other side of this is that people can feel overwhelmed by security and online threats.

In a study exploring online activities, researchers at the NIST found that more than half of the research participants referred to feelings of security fatigue. The researchers were not looking for fatigue, but they found it, with people expressing a sense of resignation, lack of control, fatalism, risk minimisation and decision avoidance. What is unsurprising, but very important, is that the research also found that this sense of security fatigue led to individuals engaging in less secure behaviours (Stanton et al., 2016). This clearly shows that awareness of cybersecurity can actually undermine security behaviours, which in turn will of course reflect in a less mature cybersecurity culture.

Awareness, in and of itself, should not be accepted as automatically good: when it comes to awareness-raising, it is not so much what you do that matters, but rather how you do it. The study identified three evidenced ways in which we can ease security fatigue and help people have more secure behaviours. They are:

- limit the number of security decisions users need to make;
- make it simple for users to choose the right security action;
- design for consistent decision making whenever possible (Stanton et al., 2016).

These recommendations highlight that, when considering the human side of cybersecurity, we need to look at system design and opportunities for using technology to support individuals, as much as we consider how to raise awareness. Security fatigue can be in response to poor security system design and cognitive overload. Minimising security fatigue relies on us making security easier, and on better communicating security messages.

When discussing cybersecurity awareness, a common question that often arises is how frequently an organisation should deliver cybersecurity awareness-raising. If awareness-raising is too often, you risk adding to security fatigue and turning your messages into noise, but if you make it too infrequent then you risk being ineffective. Like everything in cybersecurity, there is no silver bullet for this; tailoring your security awareness, behaviour and culture strategy and activities to your organisational culture is going to be more successful than trying to 'lift and shift' a one-size-fits-all approach.

However, when mapping out a security awareness programme, there are some fundamental elements to consider. Annual training is common in lots of organisations, with many capitalising on Cybersecurity Awareness Month in October to have a big push on awareness and make an impact on the organisation as a whole with engaging, innovative and informative activities. Beyond this, there are some other core awareness-raising opportunities, particularly at induction training for new employees and targeted training for high-risk groups and those who need cybersecurity training as a core requirement of their position. Having on-demand, bite-sized content is a fantastic way of supporting your colleagues, so they can get answers to security questions as they arise; cybersecurity champions, discussed in the previous chapter, can also really help with this.

When planning your awareness programme, think about it from the perspective of the colleagues you are trying to support with this programme. Consult your colleagues throughout the organisation, for example via your champions or via focus groups with a varied cross-section of areas and levels of the organisation. What content would help them and when would it be most effective to deliver that content? For example, you may want to deliver awareness-raising that coincides with holidays and celebrations, relevant to people's personal and family lives as well as their role in the workplace.

KNOW YOUR AUDIENCE

The importance of understanding your audience and making awareness-raising activities relevant to them has already been covered in the discussion in the 'Enabling Self-Efficacy' section. Knowing your audience means making the content relevant to the people in the room, using examples that will resonate with them, and it also means speaking their language. Cybersecurity is rife with technical jargon. When we communicate with people using terms that they do not understand, we are failing to make the messages relevant to them and we are likely to alienate them. Define the terms that you are using, such as 'password manager', 'two-factor authentication', 'spear-phishing' and 'ransomware'; perhaps provide a glossary of terms.

Also consider how you can speak the language of your audience. For example, if you are delivering awareness-raising to the board, focus on the business implications of cybersecurity risks, rather than the technical issues. Board members are generally more attuned to business and financial risk than cybersecurity risks, so by discussing cybersecurity in terms of potential financial and reputation damage, you are speaking to board members on a level that is more comfortable and relevant to them. Highlight the business aspects of cybersecurity as opposed to the technical ones; for example, when discussing incident response, you can focus on the impact an incident would have on customers, on reputation and on different parts of the organisation, such as PR and communications, human relations (HR) and the legal teams. Rather than considering what you want to say, consider your messages in light of what your audience needs to hear and how you can most effectively shape your communications to achieve that.

How we communicate cybersecurity messages is a fundamental factor in the extent to which we successfully raise awareness of cybersecurity. By success, I mean the extent to which people listen to our messaging, understand what we have to say and, as a result, pursue more secure behaviours, in turn contributing to the development of a more positive cybersecurity culture.

SUMMARY

Awareness-raising does not exist in a vacuum and the end-goal of awareness-raising activities should not simply be that people are more aware of cybersecurity. The end-goal of raising awareness should be that people have a better understanding of cybersecurity and that they are therefore engaging in behaviours that will better protect themselves and the organisation, supporting a positive and mature cybersecurity culture:

> Knowledge and awareness is a prerequisite to change behaviour but not necessarily sufficient ... It is very important to embed positive cybersecurity behaviours, which can result to thinking becoming a habit, and a part of an organisation's cybersecurity culture.
>
> (Bada et al., 2015)

We will move on to explore cybersecurity behaviour and culture in the rest of this book.

NEXT STEPS

Let's take a look at some next steps that you can consider in terms of cybersecurity awareness in your organisation:

- Review your awareness-raising activities or plans with the idea of experiential learning in mind: could you utilise live demonstrations or tabletop exercises to bring cybersecurity to life?

- How interactive is your awareness-raising? What can you do to encourage people to become active, not just passive, participants (for example using the modified Feynman technique)?

- Review the messaging in your awareness-raising, and try to create a mechanism to sense-check it with non-security colleagues, for example with a focus group that explores the following questions:

  - Does the language used in your awareness-raising encourage people to feel comfortable, confident and psychologically safe?

  - Do your non-security colleagues relate to the language used or is there technical jargon that creates a barrier and would be better removed or more clearly defined?

- Review your awareness-raising activities to identify which category they fall into from the Accelerated Learning framework: somatic, auditory, visual and intellectual. Aim for a cross-section of all the different methods.

- Consider whether awareness-raising content in your organisation tackles threats in a responsible way that focuses on efficacy messages – using fear carefully – or whether it wields fear as a blunt tool, which is more likely to backfire than positively contribute to awareness, behaviour and culture.

- Does your organisation's approach to security recognise security fatigue and the need for good system design and user-friendly technology? Or is awareness seen as a panacea to solve all aspects of how people interact with technology?

4 UNDERSTANDING BEHAVIOUR

Ciarán Mc Mahon

A core element in securing business information systems is appreciating how the users of those systems interact with them. Consequently, in this chapter we are going to discuss how to understand cybersecurity behaviour and try to gain insight into what is happening with this on a psychological level.

It is important that we spend time trying to understand the nuances of our colleagues' mental, emotional and social processes if we are to encourage them to be more security conscious. As such, this chapter will lay the foundations for changing cybersecurity behaviours, which we will cover in Chapter 5.

This chapter first looks at some examples of how cybersecurity behaviour is defined. The idea here is to tease these definitions apart in order to get a better sense of how tricky it can be to accurately describe what we are interested in, and also to try to relate them to cybersecurity in practice. Ultimately what we are trying to do is to get a clear picture of what we mean by 'cybersecurity behaviour' – what is relevant, and what can be ruled out.

Second, we will examine some theories of human psychology; here we will try to get to grips with how psychological science operates and to see how its theories can be applied to a cybersecurity context. This will involve studying the theories most commonly used to explain cybersecurity behaviour in academic research. Additionally, we will show how these theories can be applied in practice by illustrating them through some potential workplace scenarios.

Third, we will investigate the basics of studying cybersecurity behaviour. This will involve examining social science research methods and seeing how they can be applied to a cybersecurity context. As such, this means discussing things like hypothesis development and research design. There are lots of different methods that can be used here, depending on which behaviours we are interested in. So, in this section we will discuss the relative advantages and disadvantages of deploying tools like surveys, focus groups and interviews when trying to understand cybersecurity behaviour.

> Throughout this chapter and the next we will discuss a survey carried out by the authors at the (ISC)[2] Secure Summits in 2017. During workshops at conferences in Amsterdam, Stockholm, Zurich and London, over a hundred senior information security professionals gave us some fascinating insight into working with end user cybersecurity behaviour.

Finally, this chapter will conclude with a list of concrete next steps for you to follow as you try to better understand your own professional context. These actions are designed to ease you into getting to grips with behaviour without changing too much too soon.

DEFINING SECURITY BEHAVIOUR

When we say, 'cybersecurity behaviour', or 'information security behaviour' what exactly do we mean? In the modern office environment, almost every behaviour has a digital element and is therefore vulnerable to error or compromise. In that light, nearly everything that today's employee does could conceivably fall under that heading. Yet at the same time, security professionals instinctively know what they are concerned about. You know risky behaviour when you see it, don't you? But how do we take that implicit knowledge, and formulate it into something that can be used, and indeed reproduced?

First, let's take a look at this useful definition published in the journal *Computers & Security* by a professor of computing at the University of South Africa:

> Compliant information security behavior refers to the set of core information security activities that have to be adhered to by end-users to maintain information security as defined by information security policies.
>
> (Padayachee, 2012)

Note how this definition does not actually mention any specific behaviours, it merely mentions 'security activities' – the implication being that we should already know what those are. It further says that these activities not only should be adhered to by end users, but that they are 'defined by information security policies'. This should be our first important lesson in understanding cybersecurity behaviour.

Security professionals may be interested in a given end user behaviour. Or perhaps more accurately, ordered to put a stop to a given behaviour.

However, rather than trying to understand what's going on in your colleagues' minds when they are carrying out this behaviour, it is wise to first look at existing information security policies. Is this problematic behaviour explicitly forbidden?

In other words, you can't blame people for doing something wrong, if it has not already been clearly specified as wrong. Of course, there may be gaps here, but at the very least, this should be your first port of call when trying to understand user behaviour.

Let's take a look at another academic definition of cybersecurity behaviour. This one comes from a team of Australian researchers:

> Human behaviours that may put an organisation at risk include inadvertently or deliberately divulging passwords to others, falling victim to phishing emails by clicking on embedded web site links, or inserting non-familiar media into work or home computers.
>
> (Parsons et al., 2014)

This probably looks a lot more familiar to the average security professional: there are lots of things that we don't want users to do. Don't use a weak password, don't leave your workstation unlocked – lots of don'ts. But while this is probably more recognisable, it should not really sit comfortably with us. The question remains, what is good cybersecurity behaviour? You can tell the end users what not to do, but can you tell them what to do?

When we are trying to understand cybersecurity behaviour, we should try to bear in mind a number of lessons from this exercise in trying to define it. First, while we may be professionally interested or concerned about a particular behaviour that is occurring in our workplace, we should first ask whether or not it is actually contrary to our organisation's information security policy. If not, why not? What is the process involved in changing that, and informing end users of that change? How do we create good 'rule books' that end users can understand and have input to, and that can adapt to rapidly evolving technological environments?

Second, security professionals are often mostly interested in preventing users from doing harmful or risky things – 'don't do this', 'don't do that'. Do you think that this kind of negative awareness-raising can be successful in the long term? As described in the last chapter, we have to be careful when we use fear in the context of cybersecurity.

Third, we need to reflect on what we are most concerned with here. Note the line of commonality between the two definitions: involving the end user in reducing the risk to the organisation. How do we do that? Recall also the advice in the previous chapter about knowing your audience and making your content relevant to them.

In sum, remember to specify as clearly as possible what behaviours you want users to do, and not to do, and to make sure these are included in organisational policy documentation. In Chapter 5 we will go into more detail regarding the types of specific behaviours you may be interested in – such as choosing strong passwords and not being fooled by phishing emails – but for now we will continue to focus on trying to better understand behaviour generally.

THEORIES OF SECURITY BEHAVIOUR

Because research into the human aspects of cybersecurity behaviour is still largely in its infancy, theories specifically written to understand this context are few and far between. Instead, what is more common is that theories from wider social science are interpreted in a cybersecurity context. For the most part, cybersecurity behaviour research has been carried out with regard to two particular theories. Each of these has its own particular strengths and weaknesses in helping us to understand end user behaviour so we will go through them one by one. In comparing and contrasting them, we will get closer to understanding the psychology of the end user and better at involving them in protecting their organisation. Furthermore, both these theories will be explained with illustration to common cybersecurity behaviours, in order to show you how you can better understand your end users' difficulties.

Theory of planned behaviour

The theory of planned behaviour (Ajzen, 1991) originates in studies of interpersonal persuasion but is now used widely across the social sciences, including studies of cybersecurity. The basic idea with this theory is that when trying to understand why a person carries out any behaviour, we must think about their intentions around that behaviour. Moreover, their intention to act or not to act is composed of attitudes pertaining to that behaviour.

First, a person's behaviour is influenced by their attitude to the behaviour – how they feel about it, whether or not they think it is a good thing to do and so on. Second, it is influenced by what are known as subjective norms, or whether or not the behaviour is common, or something that everyone else is doing. And finally, it is influenced by perceived behavioural control – or how easy the individual thinks the behaviour is to carry out. Furthermore, these factors interact with each other in a number of interesting ways.

So, for example, let's take a given behaviour in a cybersecurity context – such as locking the screen of your computer when leaving your desk. We all know we should do this, but often we don't. According to the theory of planned behaviour, this could be because of a number of reasons. In the case of behavioural attitude, it might simply be that we don't like locking our computer or feel that it is unimportant. In the case of subjective norms, it could be that none of our co-workers bothers locking their computers, so we don't feel like we need to either. And in the case of perceived behavioural control, it might simply be that we feel that locking our workstation is a pain – perhaps our password is too long and complicated, and we don't like having to type it in so often.

More to the point, in any given context, while a person's attitude and subjective norms are important, their perceived behavioural control is the critical one. For example, say we dislike locking our workstation every time we step away from our desk, and also believe that it is pointless (low attitude to the behaviour), and maybe we can see that none of our colleagues locks theirs (low subjective norms). However, if at the same time we think that we are capable of doing it easily and effectively (high perceived behavioural control), then it is possible that we will still actually lock our workstation regularly.

On the other hand, take password behaviour. Imagine a person who knows that password security is important and is a good thing (high attitude to the behaviour). And they know that there is a lot of pressure to maintain good password security within their organisation (high social norms). But imagine also that this person does not think that they are capable of remembering their new password (low perceived behavioural control). In this case, despite the former two factors, I suspect we are likely to see passwords written on sticky notes. As such, the crucial point to take from the theory of planned behaviour is that not only do we have to work on positive attitudes to cybersecurity behaviours, and improving social norms around them too, but, fundamentally, we have to convince end users that they are actually capable of executing these behaviours too.

Protection motivation theory

In contrast, the protection motivation theory (Rogers, 1975) originated in the health sector, and has been more used around issues like exercise, lifestyle and also cancer prevention and alcohol consumption. What it is essentially concerned with is how people respond to warnings telling them not to do certain things – such as eat unhealthy food or smoke cigarettes. As such, you can see how it can fit in with the kind of fear-based messaging that is common in the information security profession. So how does it explain how end users should react to this kind of messaging?

The protection motivation theory posits that an individual's behaviour when encountering fear-based warnings is influenced by, on the one hand, their threat appraisal, and on the other hand, their coping appraisal. These two elements both comprise three further factors each. So, a person's threat appraisals comprise the following assessments: how severe the threat is, how vulnerable they personally are to it, and how valuable the rewards are that they will lose if they follow the warning. In contrast, a person's coping appraisal comprises another batch of assessments: how effective their response to the threat is likely to be, how much they can actually cope with the threat, and how much their response will cost them.

For example, let's imagine that you are messaging users that they must install security updates. You warn them that they risk compromising their device by not doing so. However, the protection motivation theory might posit an individual's thought response as follows. In terms of threat appraisal, they might agree that the threat is severe, and that they themselves are vulnerable to it. However, they may decide that if they do not install the updates, they could be working instead and deem this to be too valuable an activity to lose. And in terms of coping appraisal, this individual may think that their response to the threat would be ineffective and that they would be unable to cope with it if it happened, but that the act of installing the updates will cost them too much effort.

Now in this theory, there is no superior factor, unlike with perceived behavioural intention in the theory of planned behaviour above. But it does make you think about what might be happening psychologically in your work environment. Let's break down your colleagues' reaction to your fear-based messaging:

1. I agree that the threats are severe.
2. I agree my device(s) may be vulnerable.
3. But anything I do will be ineffective because the threats are so severe.
4. If something does go wrong, I have no idea what to do; I won't be able to cope.
5. I will have to spend time on trying to do something that won't really help me (see three and four above).

So, how will they react? In all probability, they'll make the decision that what you're asking them to do will take too much time, require too much effort and won't change a thing. Thus, they won't run the update. As a result, you've been wasting your time too.

To be clear, you don't need to start testing these theories in your workplace, and it isn't necessarily important either to pick one or the other. The point is to try to get to grips with the psychological processes that may underlie your end users' behaviours. Think about what could possibly motivate them. What are their intentions? What are they afraid of? What do they think is normal? What do they think they are capable of? Asking yourself questions like these is an important step to understanding cybersecurity behaviour.

MEASURING BEHAVIOUR

These days in professional working environments, measurement is key. 'If you can't measure it, you can't manage it' seems to be the modern management mantra. Consequently, security professionals dealing with improving end user cybersecurity behaviour will usually be tasked with somehow first benchmarking and then improving these numbers. That's the idea: measure the behaviour, intervene somehow and then measure the behaviour again, with hopefully improved numbers. But, as social scientists have been realising for many years, measuring human activity is a tricky business.

As everyone working in this sector will appreciate, getting reliable and valid measures of security compliance is difficult, but there are a number of tools that can be used in this regard. For example, in our Secure Summits survey of 2017, we used a variety of methods to understand participants' understanding and experience of the information security industry. Before each workshop, participants were contacted and asked if they had any specific questions or challenges. This kind of 'fishing exercise' allowed us to get a sense of what was important to the security professionals we were going to be working with and prepare accordingly. It might not have given us a completely accurate reflection of what every participant was interested in, but that's not the point – it gave us a rough indication of what to expect: what people felt strongly enough about to type out before coming to the workshop itself. In other words, sometimes you don't need to measure user behaviour per se, sometimes you just need to get a sense of what they are experiencing and feeling. Those early responses then fed into the drafting of the questions we asked them in the survey.

The survey was carried out at each of the four (ISC)² Secure Summits in 2017, with 118 responses in total: 33 in Amsterdam, 17 in Stockholm, 18 in Zurich and 50 in London. As you can see from Figure 4.1, most of these participants were highly experienced information security professionals.

Additionally, you can see from Figure 4.2 that our respondents comprised a good mix of technical versus managerial roles, with many holding dual positions. Consequently, we are confident that the responses to the survey represent a good indication of the current state of the art in how security professionals deal with human factors in their roles.

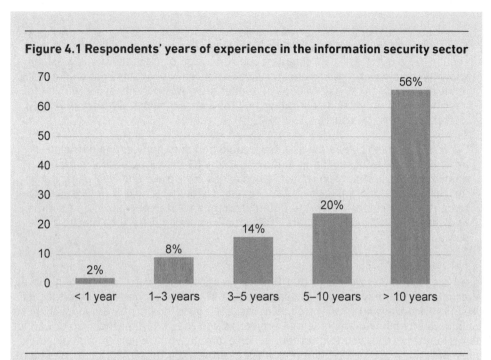

Figure 4.1 Respondents' years of experience in the information security sector

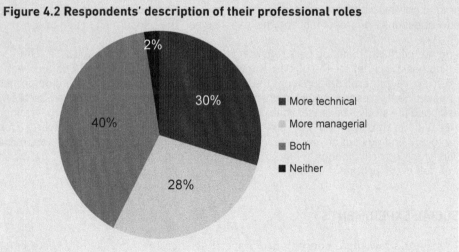

Figure 4.2 Respondents' description of their professional roles

- More technical
- More managerial
- Both
- Neither

A key point in social science methodologies, such as surveys, is to only ask questions that you need to know the answer to. For example, in the 'About You' section we did not ask participants about their age or gender. This is because knowing the answer to those questions does not really shed any light on the rest of the data. This isn't to say that age or gender are not important issues within the information security sector, but rather that they were not what we were primarily interested in with this survey.

Good research ethics like this has the double bonus of not wasting participants' time, and also reducing the amount of personally identifiable information you gather, and hence minimising data protection risk. Hence, we didn't ask participants for their email address either. As a result, it would be next to impossible to reidentify participants from the data set. You can save your participants' time and save yourself a General Data Protection Regulation (GDPR) headache at the same time.

In a practical sense, we found that Google Forms worked very well for our survey. Alternatively, you may have an internal product of choice, or there are other services like SurveyMonkey and so on you could utilise. It is a good idea to play around with these tools before beginning any research project as you may find that they can or cannot do certain tasks that you might require. For example, with regard to multiple choice questions, there are several different ways of presenting these and it can take some time to get this right. It is good practice to ensure a certain level of consistency across how questions are presented, and this can also be time-consuming to achieve.

Another point worth noting here regarding data collection is what is known as HARKing (Hypothesizing After the Results are Known). You can see that in our 2017 data collection exercise we gathered data in four cities, so you might wonder if there were differences in participants' responses between them. But that wasn't an idea we had before we designed the study – because while cross-cultural cybersecurity might be interesting, it was not our aim here – so it doesn't make sense to look at it now. In other words, don't try to pull findings out of your data that you didn't design your study to look for. Human behaviour is tricky enough to understand without building a house of mirrors around yourself in the process.

SOCIAL EXPERIMENTS

There are a few more concepts from social science that are useful to note before trying to measure any aspect of human behaviour. Some of these may seem obvious in retrospect, having carried out a project, but it is much better to think them through before you start putting a plan in action.

On the one hand, there is what is known as the Hawthorne effect. First noticed in an industrial context in the United States in the 1930s, this refers to the fact that when being observed while they're working, people may be more productive than usual. Of course, this isn't surprising, but it has tripped up many an organisational change project over the years.

For example, you may decide that you are interested in improving a particular type of cybersecurity behaviour. As you begin attempting to measure its current level, word gets around the office. Hence, thanks to people's reactions, you record an abnormally high level of activity. Consequently, you may think that your colleagues are actually performing this behaviour at a decent level already, and not bother with your intervention to improve it. Worse still, you carry out the intervention anyway, but will be comparing it to an unrealistic baseline. Hence, you have to think of some way of recording this behaviour in as unobtrusive way as possible. Tricky, eh?

On the other hand, there is also what is known as the experimenter or observer effect. In this case, it's not so much the people being tested who react, but the person doing the testing. What happens here is that you unconsciously try to find what you go looking for. This may cause you to miss some things and over-emphasise others. Imagine you are doing a Universal Serial Bus (USB) key drop across a building in a company that you know well. In this case you should really be dropping the keys throughout the campus at random. But the fact that you know the place already may impinge on your behaviour – you already have an opinion on which teams will be good, and which will be weak on this exercise, and that knowledge can easily affect the results you achieve. You might drop more keys in the departments that you had poor relationships with, or you may over-compensate and drop none. Complicated, huh?

This is why the 'double-blind' experiment is the gold standard of human subject research. Perhaps you are interested in how many of your co-workers leave their workstations unlocked at lunchtime. To counteract the Hawthorne effect, you won't signal what is being tested – that is, you don't mention the behaviour in a company-wide email. And to counteract the observer effect, you get someone else to do the measuring – and without telling them what they're measuring. One possible method here would be to get a trainee or intern to help. You might tell them that you are interested in recording how many employees still use sticky notes. In order to do this, you need them to take photographs of everyone's workstation at lunchtime. Hence, you will get an accurate record of every computer that is unlocked, and with neither the employees' attention being sparked, nor your own observer effect biasing the results. Of course, using this method you may pick up some passwords written on the sticky notes too, but only record this behaviour if you said you were looking for this too – no HARKing, remember!

RELIABILITY AND VALIDITY

It's important you keep in mind two important features of good behavioural measurement with any such exercise. In the first case, measures should be reliable. In this context, reliability refers to the degree to which a measure will produce the same result again and again. And in the second case, measures should also be valid. Here, validity refers to the degree to which a measure actually measures what it claims to measure.

Neither of these factors on its own is good enough. For example, say my weighing scales says that I haven't put on any weight since before Christmas. Because it's giving me the same result as the last time, I presume that it's reliable. But that doesn't mean that it's valid – the scales might be jammed. Similarly, a breathalyser kit might be able to validly test the amount of alcohol in my bloodstream – but it's not reliable, as it's a single use test. However, in cybersecurity, we are not trying to measure physical or chemical quantities. We're trying to measure people, who are a lot more complicated.

A critical point here is that people can react to being tested. Always bear in mind the concept of reflexivity – people can learn or improve from how they are being tested, perhaps even try to outwit the tester.

One particularly troublesome example of this is known as the Dunning–Kruger effect. In this classic study (Kruger and Dunning, 1999), a sample drawn from the general population were given tests of basic arithmetic and general knowledge, but also asked where they expected to score compared to everyone else. Extraordinarily, those who ended up scoring lowest had expected to score in the upper end. Moreover, those who thought they would be in the midrange actually scored close to the top. In other words, the smart people were underconfident, and the overconfident were pretty dumb. As it was put more poetically by W. B. Yeats 'The best lack all conviction, while the worst / Are full of passionate intensity' ('The Second Coming', 1920).

Perhaps you've come across this in infosec? The person who loudly proclaims that they 'know all of this stuff' and therefore doesn't need to attend your cybersecurity awareness workshop? And later it transpires that in reality they have the riskiest behaviours of all? In fact, in the next chapter we will discuss a number of scientific research papers that suggest something like this at work in certain cybersecurity contexts and consider how to deal with it. As such, the Dunning–Kruger effect is something that I suspect many of you reading this book will recognise. Don't be misled!

RESEARCH METHODS

When we start putting a plan in place to try to understand the security behaviour of our end users, we have to be careful and also a little cunning. First, we have to formulate the problem as precisely as possible: what exactly is the behaviour we are interested in? What exactly is the problem? This can only come from carefully observing the context you are interested in – don't simply start off trying to change things without understanding and describing what is happening. In particular, at this point you should try to define what you are interested in, and what you are not interested in.

So, for example, you may decide that you are only concerned with behaviour that occurs within your organisation's premises, on its workstations and during office hours. That doesn't mean that what employees do on their smartphones on their commute home isn't important, it just means that for the purpose of this current exercise, you have put it to one side for the time being. Mission creep is a problem all over industry, but when you are attempting to scientifically understand human behaviour, not only can it mean you will likely end up gathering more personal information than you need, but it will be much more difficult to interpret what is actually happening in the data you acquire.

Second, after formulating the problem and limiting your areas of interest, we need to generate a hypothesis. A hypothesis is the scientist's version of a bet. Because X is happening, if we do Y, Z will occur. The critical aspect of a hypothesis is not that it 'comes true', but that there is a distinct possibility that it may not come true. In other words, when your hypothesis is written down, it can be clearly seen that it can be falsified. It's not 'this person will never do that', it's more like 'this person will not do that within the next month'.

Hence a hypothesis is similar to an acronym you might have come across before: SMART. This usually stands for something like specific, measurable, achievable, relevant and time-bound. We might say something like: 'employees who take this training session will, on average, click on 50 per cent fewer phishing links over the following week'. By spelling it out precisely like this, you have clear pass or fail states (which is clearly of benefit to management). Notably, to accurately test this hypothesis you need to be able to compare this group to something else. That could be themselves the previous month (bearing in mind the Hawthorne and observer effects mentioned above), or you could use a control group: another bunch of people who are, to all intents and purposes, the same as the group that you give the training to. The latter option would be preferred scientifically, but managers tend not to like spending money on half their workforce not getting trained. Again, there are practical limitations to what you can achieve in even the most well-resourced organisations.

Moreover, you can now see why scientists also use what is known as the null hypothesis: clearly describing the default position, where nothing of significance has happened. In this case, we can say that the null hypothesis would be something like: having taken this training session employees will, on average click on less than 50 per cent fewer phishing links over the following week. Note the null hypothesis does not say the training session will have no effect. Rather, it gives a specific and measurable method for ascertaining what will be deemed to be a significant effect. In social science there are statistical methods for this but in your case you will likely have to make a business decision as to what is a meaningful result. Hence, we distinguish a 'test hypothesis' from the 'null hypothesis' in order to be able to clearly state when interventions, such as a training session, have not been effective.

Third, we need to choose an experimental design. This choice will be influenced largely by how much we think we already understand the behaviour we are interested in. So, for example, if you think you know what particular type of training will reduce the amount of phishing links that your colleagues click on, a focus group won't be much use to you. In this case, an experimental design like the one mentioned above would probably be best – that is, with a control group (who don't do anything) and an experimental group (who are receiving the new training programme).

But on the other hand, it probably wouldn't be a good idea to begin a project with an experiment. For example, if you are trying to establish what is involved when people share passwords, then a focus group first would probably be a better idea. Ultimately you have to cut your cloth to suit your measure.

The key idea I would stress here is a kind of elegance or parsimony – the best social scientists do not get lots of insight by carrying out large cumbersome projects with many concepts and lots of moving parts. Rather they use very simple, economical and well-thought-out research designs. You don't have to reinvent the wheel; you just have to drill down carefully into what is most important to you, and what you can do with the tools at your disposal.

While information security professionals typically favour penetration testing methods such as USB key drops and phishing tools, there are many other, less dramatic, methods that can be used to get a very good sense of end user behaviour. These include straightforward online survey or questionnaire methods.

You may also find that it might be useful to go beyond simply measuring end user behaviour. Social science tries to overcome limitations in quantitative data by using qualitative research methods. These are methods where we are not merely trying to gather statistical evidence of the behaviour we're interested in, but also to gather more context, language and description of the behaviour.

In other words, qualitative research involves interviews or focus groups – or even something very basic like putting an open text box at the end of a survey form for respondents to type in whatever they like. This tactic can be very good for picking up answers to questions that you might not have asked – things beyond the obvious. Take, for example, suggestion boxes. Of all the professions, surely those working in cybersecurity should appreciate the value of anonymous communication? Such tools can be very useful in revealing motivations and experiences that users might not talk about otherwise.

SUMMARY

In concluding this chapter let's summarise what we have covered in trying to understand cybersecurity behaviour. We began by examining some definitions of cybersecurity behaviour and trying to decipher what these meant in terms of practical applications and policy enforcement. This moved the discussion to theories of human psychology and how they can be applied to the cybersecurity context – namely the theory of planned behaviour and the protection motivation theory. Following this we laid out the practicalities of measuring cybersecurity behaviour, and the complexities of carrying out research on human participants. We also discussed a variety of research methods and key concepts to bear in mind before setting out to analyse cybersecurity behaviour in a workplace.

NEXT STEPS

Let's round up this chapter with key action points for you to put into practice in your own professional environment. You can start with some fairly simple steps towards better understanding your colleagues' cybersecurity behaviour in your workplace without reinventing the wheel:

- Take a look at your organisation's information security policy documents. What behaviours are explicitly mentioned or prohibited?

- Find out what internal research or studies have already been carried out in your workplace. What were the findings? What was the upshot of the project?

- Try drafting an internal survey of cybersecurity behaviour and compliance, based on previous research or audits carried out in your organisation.

- Take a given cybersecurity behaviour that currently occurs in your organisation. Can you formulate it clearly and precisely? Can you develop a test hypothesis, and a null hypothesis?

- More to the point, can you interpret what is happening here in relation to the theory of planned behaviour, and also in relation to the protection motivation theory? Do they make for different or similar predictions?

- Draw up a plan for how you would carry out a focus group with end users in your workplace. How would you structure it? Who would facilitate it? What would the topic be? How would you record participants' input?

- How could you carry out an anonymous feedback submission system in your workplace? How would you ensure that your colleagues can trust that if they use it, their identities cannot be revealed to senior management?

5   CHANGING BEHAVIOUR

Ciarán Mc Mahon

In this second chapter on information security behaviour, our focus moves from understanding behaviour to changing behaviour. It isn't enough to comprehend why our colleagues and co-workers act in certain ways; we also need to be able to improve their performance. In other words, having gained some insight into what is happening on a psychological level, we now must try to use that knowledge to direct their behaviour in a more security conscious direction.

As such, this chapter is structured with regard to the most recognisable cybersecurity areas, where we most often require end users to change their behaviour. In each of the areas described, you will be presented with ideas that you can apply to your own workplace, which include published scientific research and findings from our workshops.

However, per the last chapter, it isn't really very useful to talk about 'cybersecurity behaviour' in general. That might be the case in academic theory, but not in everyday practice. If your superiors task you with 'improving cybersecurity' in the workforce, then you will be hard-pressed to achieve success. You need to focus on specific cybersecurity behaviours if you are going to change anything for the better.

That means that this chapter will include sections on access control, password management, anti-phishing, workstation locking, removable media and mobile security, updating, and anti-virus. Admittedly, this doesn't cover every aspect of end user security activity, and arguably some aspects are more important than others, but it is hoped that this broad overview will give you a good foundation from which to start changing particular behaviours in your workplace.

INFORMATION SECURITY POLICY

First, once again it is worth discussing a little policy before we begin. At the outset, based on the Next steps section of the previous chapter, we're assuming that you have had a good look at your organisation's policy documents, and made certain recommendations about what is and isn't included. Whatever behaviour we are interested in changing, we need end users to be more aware of their organisation's information security policy than they currently are, not to mention following it, and contributing to it. Crucially, we also need end users to report incidents to their information security team.

In the Secure Summits survey of 2017, we asked participants about behaviour and policy. As mentioned in Chapter 4, these are intimately linked. Essentially, it is unfair to criticise end users for doing something incorrectly, if that behaviour has not been explicitly prohibited. It therefore is essential that end users are aware of their organisation's information security policies, and what behaviours are disallowed by them.

From our survey results, it seems that the InfoSec community has some work to do here. When presented with the following statement, our participants responded as follows:

Every end user in my organisation knows which behaviours are violations of information security policy:

Strongly disagree	7%
Disagree	25%
Neither agree nor disagree	25%
Agree	40%
Strongly agree	3%

That's a stark figure: only 3 per cent of information security professionals could 'strongly agree' that their end users knew which behaviours were violations of policy. Similarly, a total of 32 per cent disagreed or strongly disagreed with the statement. This supports the idea that the very first step we have to address in changing end user security behaviour is simply educating them about their organisation's information security policy, and what behaviours it prohibits.

At the same time, when we asked participants a related question, we received more heartening results:

My organisation has a clear, simple and effective process for reporting cybersecurity incidents:

Strongly disagree	3%
Disagree	11%
Neither agree nor disagree	27%
Agree	41%
Strongly agree	18%

So, with nearly 60 per cent of respondents agreeing or strongly agreeing that their organisation has a good process for reporting incidents, we get to see where information security professionals' priorities lie: less on policy, more on process. This would suggest that we need to do more work on educating end users about which behaviours are forbidden (and why) rather than on reporting those behaviours.

However, when we asked security professionals about the sort of incidents that such processes are designed to defend against, the results were not exactly encouraging:

End user errors or violations of information security policy are certain to be detected:

Strongly disagree	10%
Disagree	31%
Neither agree nor disagree	40%
Agree	17%
Strongly agree	2%

Less than 20 per cent of respondents could agree that violations of policy in their organisation would be certain to be detected. In a way, this isn't surprising – maintaining absolute visibility over an internal network, not to mention all human behaviour in an organisation too, is a tall order. But nevertheless, it does reflect the scale of the task in front of us. And to carry out that task – of defending our organisations to the best of our ability – we need our fellow end users to work with us. You might say that the best way to improve the information security team's visibility over the network is to actually involve the end users as another line of defence.

In that regard, we also asked our respondents about the system of justice in their organisation with regard to information security policy violations:

End user errors or violations are disciplined fairly and transparently, regardless of seniority:

Strongly disagree	11%
Disagree	24%
Neither agree nor disagree	36%
Agree	25%
Strongly agree	4%

These results are exceptionally concerning from an organisational psychology perspective. Less than 30 per cent of the information security professionals we surveyed could agree that errors and violations were dealt with fairly by their employers. That is a disappointing and worrying statistic, as getting end users involved with positive information security behaviour requires, as an essential element, their understanding that their mistakes will be handled impartially.

A couple of research studies are worth discussing here. There is one carried out by a Canadian team of researchers in 2009 that is a good starting point in examining how user behaviour is linked to organisational policy, and ultimately culture. Bulgurcu, Cavusoglu and Benbasat (2009) used the theory of planned behaviour, which you will recall from Chapter 4, to examine what factors influenced whether or not employees intended to comply with their information security policies. This study used a panel of 464 adults resident in the United States, employed by a diverse set of organisations.

In the light of that theory, and the answers to the first question in our Secure Summits survey above, it is probably unsurprising that Bulgurcu and colleagues found that participants' awareness of information security positively predicted their attitude to comply with their organisation's policies. In other words, generally speaking, the more someone is aware of information security and information security policies, the more likely they are to comply with policies. So, not exactly surprising. But Bulgurcu et al. also asked their participants about another factor: how fair they thought those policies were. This proved to be an equally powerful predictor of attitudes and intention to comply with information security policy. In other words, users are more likely to comply with policies that they feel are fair and transparent.

This paper concluded that 'creating a fair environment and ensuring procedural justice in regards to implementing security rules and regulations is the key to effective information security management' (Bulgurcu et al., 2009, p. 3273). We can't expect to change users' behaviour in a more positive way if they do not feel that they are treated impartially.

However, let's look in the mirror for a minute, too. Another study of interest comes from Ashenden and Sasse, published in 2013. Again, as with the previous paper, the industry may have changed since then, but its insights have stood the test of time. This team of UK researchers used a qualitative methodology and conducted in-depth, semi-structured interviews with CISOs working at large international organisations. Strikingly, this paper is sub-titled: 'Their own worst enemy?' which gives you some idea as to its findings.

In these interviews, Ashenden and Sasse were primarily interested in information security awareness campaigns, and how CISOs used them to effect cultural change – in other words, a large chunk of what this book is also about. Among the many themes that emerged in these interviews, including issues around business strategy and marketing, those that are most striking centre on the CISOs' struggle to gain credibility. Ashenden and Sasse surmise that this is because CISOs seem to lack organisational power, experience a certain amount of confusion about their role identity and are often unable to engage effectively with employees. Crucially, the researchers point out that while each of the interviewees worked at large organisations that were perceived to be at the forefront of information security practice, none of them had a clear idea whether or not their awareness-raising activities and tools actually had any effect in changing end user behaviour, despite spending lots of time promoting them. Ashenden and Sasse liken this to parents giving children toys and pizza simply to keep them quiet.

As such, let your #1 take-home message from this part of the book be to interact with end users more: try to understand what they think is fair, and what they think works – this is the only way you will know whether or not your efforts to change behaviour are actually working. More to the point, this is a crucial part of practice in developing and updating your organisation's information security policy – if end users are consulted about it, they are more likely to adhere to it.

TECHNIQUES FOR CHANGING BEHAVIOUR

There are a number of basic techniques at your disposal as a security professional in trying to change the behaviour of your colleagues. In the examples that follow, I have made particular recommendations as to which to use in particular circumstances. However, your mileage may vary: these techniques will have varying efficacy in different organisational contexts. This is not an exact science: think of yourself as an artist or an engineer trying to choose the right tool for the job at hand, rather than pointlessly searching for a magic bullet that doesn't exist.

Automated tools

First, as you surely know, there are automated tools. These essentially force users to execute certain behaviours or prevent them from doing things. For example, you could conceivably run a script over the network to log out every workstation after, say, three minutes of inactivity. The advantages of such tools are that they are very cheap, will work all day, every day and equally apply across every level of seniority.

However, if these tools are not perceived to be fair, you can be sure that someone will try to find a way around them. Take the auto-log-out script mentioned above. Three minutes might be seen as an unreasonably short period of time. I've heard of employees using all kinds of vibrating contraptions to keep their mouse moving while they were away from their desk – all so that they don't have to suffer the indignity of having to re-enter their password. Consequently, you might come under pressure to increase the time limit to 5, 6 or even 10 minutes. Which may actually defeat the purpose of the script in the first place, and back to square one we go!

Human behavioural tools

Second, there are human behavioural tools – namely, the carrot and the stick. On the one hand, when a user does something that we don't want them to do, we can punish them, in order to try to convince them not to do it again. On the other hand, when they do the right thing, we can reward them, in order to encourage them to do it more often.

To be frank, in the security industry there is way too much of the former, whereas the latter has long been preferred by psychological scientists and practitioners. That is, instead of trying to stop users from doing 'bad things', we should try to encourage them to do 'good things'.

Crucially, there are positive and negative variations of both of these – in psychological science this is known as operant, or instrumental, conditioning. For example, a negative punishment would involve removing something from the user in order to discourage them from performing a particular behaviour again. Whereas, alternatively, a positive reinforcement would mean giving the subject something in order to convince them to repeat a behaviour.

Furthermore, it is worth noting that in terms of both punishment and reinforcement, we can talk about both formal and informal procedures. Some behaviour is serious enough to merit written organisational policy documentation, whereas others can be handled unofficially. Again, this is a kind of toolbox you can pick and choose from, depending on the security behaviour you are interested in at any given time. Let's sketch this out with a few examples in Table 5.1 to make it a bit clearer.

It is crucial to note that with any of these behavioural techniques, for them to be effective, they must act like the automatic tools mentioned previously. In other words, they must be applied both immediately and consistently. I must stress, however, that

Table 5.1 Types of operant conditioning, with formal and informal examples

Type of operant conditioning	Type of procedure	Punishment (trying to decrease a behaviour)	Reinforcement (trying to increase a behaviour)
Positive (adding or providing something extra)	Formal	Sanctioned with additional unpleasant duties	Salary bonus
	Informal	Scolding or rebuking employee	Cake/pizza/beer
Negative (removing or eliminating something)	Formal	Docked a day's pay	Extra day of annual leave
	Informal	Taken off favourite project	Exempted from workshop attendance

while punishment certainly has its place, in general it is not preferred by behavioural scientists. And while there is a certain amount of sentimentality involved in that preference, it also boils down to efficacy: when a positive punishment is removed or a negative punishment is restored, the unwanted behaviour will often return. This is less the case with reinforcements of either kind. As such, CISOs should simply think 'less stick, more carrot' if they want to change end user behaviour in the long run.

Specific cybersecurity behaviours

Now let's examine the core areas of cybersecurity behaviour in detail. In the subsections that follow, I have drawn on the advice outlined in Coventry et al. (2014). In this report on trying to improve cybersecurity practices in the general public, published by the UK Government Office for Science, the authors proposed the following basic advice that everyone should follow:

- Use strong passwords and manage them securely.
- Use anti-virus software and firewalls.
- Log out of sites after you have finished and shut down your computer.
- Use only trusted and secure connections, computers and devices (including Wireless Fidelity (Wi-Fi)).
- Use only trusted and secure sites and services.
- Stay informed about risks (knowledge, common sense, intuition). Try to avoid scams and phishing.
- Always opt to provide the minimal amount of personal information needed for any online interaction and keep your identity protected.
- Be aware of your physical surroundings when online.
- Report cybercrimes and criminals to the authorities (Coventry et al., 2014).

Most likely, none of this advice will be unfamiliar to anyone working in cybersecurity. However, as our data shows, in training some of these pointers are more commonly focused on than others.

In the Secure Summits survey of 2017, we asked respondents which aspects of security user behaviour they focused on most in training. As you can see from Table 5.2, there is considerable variation across these specific behaviours in terms of how often they are addressed. This should give the CISO some pause for thought: are we trying to change the behaviours that are actually the riskiest to our organisations? Or simply the ones that are easiest to deal with? This is something you need to think about and discuss with your board.

Table 5.2 Frequency of inclusion of cybersecurity behaviours in user training by information security professionals

Frequency	Never	Rarely	Sometimes	Often	Constantly
Access control	3%	14%	40%	33%	10%
Workstation locking	0%	14%	28%	40%	18%
Password management	0%	5%	24%	43%	28%
Anti-phishing	1%	4%	19%	39%	37%
Removable media and mobile security	1%	13%	36%	38%	13%
Updating and patching	4%	30%	32%	22%	12%
Anti-virus and firewall	7%	28%	36%	21%	8%

Access control

At the crossover between physical security and cyber, or information security, lies access control. In the modern workplace, the behaviours we are talking about here include maintaining good door access and key card practices, properly storing sensitive printed documentation and being wise to shoulder-surfing (i.e. an adversary literally looking over your shoulder as you enter your password or other sensitive information in order to steal it). The core behaviour we need to get through to users according to Coventry et al.'s report is to get them to be aware of their physical surroundings – not only when online, but when around sensitive information in general. In this hyperconnected world, we tend to forget that information is not purely digital. Valuable information can take the form of printed paper, which can easily be left behind or picked up by individuals with nefarious intent. Moreover, even when important documents are in digital format, they require physical security – tape backups must be under lock and key, server rooms need to be robustly secured – this is the basis of access control.

To be frank, there is very little research of any kind available to give evidence-based psychological advice here. However, it strikes me that unless the issue is of a very serious nature, then probably only informal strategies of punishment or reinforcement should be used. For example, a quick trip around a given team's office space during their lunchtime (or perhaps a colleague could do this for you while you are giving them a workshop) can reveal who follows the clear desk policy, and you can leave them a chocolate or some other treat. The dirty desks get nothing! Hence, you are rewarding good behaviour, not punishing bad. Make sure to randomise this by team too – so nobody actually knows when they will be observed: remember the Hawthorne effect from Chapter 4.

Workstation locking

Locking workstations is a behaviour that our survey indicated many security professionals are trying to change, with almost three in five of our respondents reporting that they focused on it in training either 'often' or 'constantly'.

Of course, you can double up the reinforcement of the clear desk policy mentioned above for workstation locking too: one treat or reward for a clear desk, one for workstation locked – and any other behaviours you care to reinforce.

However, I'd also like to share some advice from a workshop participant. A simple way to improve user behaviour here may require only two fingers. On a Windows computer, encourage users to get into the habit of placing their left index finger on the ⊞ key, and their right index finger on the L key, which locks their computers, as they stand up and push off their desk. On a Mac, the equivalent shortcut requires just one more key: ⌘ + Shift + Q. What we're doing here is pairing the new and desired behaviour – logging out of the workstation – with an old and familiar behaviour – standing up and pushing off from the desk.

You might call this 'muscle memory' but this is just classic psychology. In the punishment and reinforcement model mentioned earlier, a behaviour is followed by certain conditions, depending on whether or not we want it increased or diminished. Here we are doing something much simpler – less voluntary and more immediate. Instead of following the behaviour we are interested in with either a reward or a punishment, here we pair the behaviour we want the user to perform with another behaviour that they already have to do anyway – such as standing up to go to the bathroom. In theory, this means that workstation locking should then become psychologically habitual, and every time the user stands up, they should feel the need to hit the keyboard with two fingers – so long as your awareness-raising activities have been successful.

In conclusion, while you can set network policies on automatically logging users out, it is far better in the long run to simplify good security culture into small behaviours that users can incorporate into their daily routine with little fuss.

Password management

Highly popular across the industry, password management was unsurprisingly reported by over 70 per cent of our survey respondents as a training aim. This naturally reflects how crucial passwords are in cybersecurity, but also how complex its psychology is too.

In a survey carried out on 263 Brazilian adults, Pilar et al. (2012) examined some factors that are often discussed with regard to memory abilities, namely education and age. On the one hand, this research found interesting differences in password behaviour, with younger and more educated participants using longer passwords than older and less educated individuals. However, when it came to difficulty in remembering passwords, this study did not find any significant differences.

What actually did predict difficulty in password memory was simply the number of passwords that respondents used. In other words, it doesn't seem to matter much if you are old or young, educated or not, but if you have too many passwords to remember, you will struggle. In general, across the various groups, difficulties in remembering passwords seemed to steeply increase beyond five passwords. As such, Pilar and co-workers (2012) recommend mnemonics and reusing passwords by category of use. This would probably fly in the face of much practice in the cybersecurity industry, but that's what the psychological research suggests. Ultimately, it is worth bearing in mind that most people have more passwords to remember than they can probably cope with.

A UK study examined a related problem – password sharing. In a 2015 survey of 497 adults, researchers Whitty et al. were interested in the type of person most likely to engage in this behaviour. Similar to Pilar and colleagues above, this team were interested in age as a factor, but also personality characteristics and, wait for it, cybersecurity knowledge.

The results were quite surprising. Overall, a whopping 51.1 per cent of participants admitted that they shared passwords – a statistic that should make a CISO's blood run cold. Moreover, given that this is self-reported data, it's likely that the actual level of this behaviour is much higher. Lots of work to do here!

Just like the Brazilian study, expectations were confounded. Yet again, the 'forgetful old person' did not appear in the data – in fact, it was younger people who emerged as more likely to share passwords. Calling to mind the Whitty paper above, this gives us some idea about how changing password behaviour should be targeted. It isn't the case that older people are more forgetful or prone to misusing passwords and therefore need special attention. In actual fact, it's probably the younger end users that we should focus on. Improving password behaviour may seem a little daunting when you think about all the end users on your network as a whole. Consequently, it might be more worthwhile to think about segmenting them **psychologically** for different campaigns. Can you work out which of your end users need to stop reusing passwords and which ones need to use more complex passwords – and target these groups accordingly?

Moreover, calling to mind the Dunning–Kruger effect mentioned in the last chapter, Pilar and colleagues found that knowledge about cybersecurity did not distinguish between those who did and did not share passwords. In other words, people who claimed to understand cybersecurity did not actually practise cybersecurity any better than those who didn't.

Hence, when we are trying to change behaviour in our own organisations, we should not take colleagues claims of knowing about cybersecurity at face value: these people should be given as much, if not more, attention than everyone else. There are no easy solutions to dealing with the Dunning–Kruger effect as it surfaces in various aspects of trying to change cybersecurity behaviour. However, it is recommended that when engaging in any behaviour change project, you encourage an atmosphere of intellectual curiosity and humility. Cybersecurity behaviour is a field where there is always something more to learn: people should feel comfortable with answering any question with 'I don't know'.

Anti-phishing

Phishing attacks seem to be the main vector for so many cyberattacks these days, and, as a result, CISOs have to design their behaviour change projects accordingly. As shown in Table 5.2, close to four-fifths of our survey respondents reported that they concentrated on phishing in training either 'often' or 'constantly'.

Like password usage, phishing is one aspect of information security behaviour where there is relatively more scientific research. One study on phishing in 2017 is noteworthy. An American team led by Carella carried out a user study experiment with 150 university students that aimed to establish an educational standard for anti-phishing campaigns (Carella et al., 2017). Carried out over several weeks, participants received a variety of phishing email simulations and data was gathered on those emails within which they clicked on the links.

Participants were split into three groups that received different levels of anti-phishing training: a control group, which received no training at all; a presentation group, which received an in-class anti-phishing training presentation; and a documents group, who were directed to anti-phishing awareness documentation each time they clicked on a link in a simulated phishing email. Notably, the actual information received by both the presentation group and the documents group was essentially the same, only the manner of its communication differed. As you can probably deduce, the documents group were being treated with a form of positive punishment: they were being given something extra in order to try to decrease a behaviour.

Seven waves of phishing emails were sent out to each of these groups. In the first week, each group performed quite similarly, with click-through rates of over 50 per cent. This is shocking enough in and of itself – before any intervention took place, the participants were highly likely to click through on a link in a phishing email.

In the second week, the presentation group received their in-class anti-phishing training presentation. Thereafter this group's click-through rate fell substantially – for a while. In waves 2, 3 and 4, the presentation group performed in the mid-30 per cent range, but by wave 7, the final week, their click-through rate was basically back where it started from, at 50 per cent. By the end of the experiment, the presentation group was performing on anti-phishing detection at the same rate as the control group, who had received no training at all. This kind of rebound may be familiar to anyone who's ever carried out cybersecurity workshops in an attempt to change behaviour.

On the other hand, those in the documents group performed very well, with their click-through rates dropping from one week to the next. By the last wave, this group were clicking on a mere 8 per cent of links in phishing emails. Hence this method of phishing training – that is, redirecting to anti-phishing resources after clicking on a phishing link in a simulated attack – appears to have a solid scientific basis and is more effective than a classroom exercise.

However, given what we outlined above regarding the effects of punishment, one would not be surprised to find that the performance of the documents group declined once the punishment stimulus was removed. This study did not include a follow-up procedure, so we don't know how well this group performed in the weeks and months thereafter. The effect on the presentation group wore off after a couple of weeks, so perhaps it would take longer than that, but one would expect that it would wear off at some point. The key for CISOs attempting to change behaviour in this way is to have a plan that is not simply a one-off: treatment has to be repeated at regular intervals.

However, paradoxically, as engineers get better at automating the detection (and quarantining) of phishing emails, end users therefore have less material to learn from. Hence, as the network gets better at preventing phishing, the end users get worse. More to the point, given that the signal in question here – phishing emails – changes from one day to the next, phishing training will always be challenging. It is therefore crucial that CISOs remain in close contact with end users and ensure that their office is seen as approachable and engaged.

Again, with regard to policy development, and indeed also in relation to culture as will be explained in the next chapters, we need to think about phishing far more broadly than simply stopping users from clicking on links. We need to have joined up thinking from that end user right up to the boardroom; from what should happen after the risky link is actually clicked, through to how that policy is developed and who is involved in that discussion, all the way to how senior executives decide on how these risks should be managed.

Removable media and mobile security

An inescapable element of the modern office is its portability. From mobile phones to USB keys and public Wi-Fi, 21st century technology now allows us to move while we work – which presents a whole new range of cybersecurity challenges. As a result, it is unsurprising that in our survey only 1 per cent had never covered these topics in end user training.

Consequently, it is worthwhile trying to understand why, for example, users plug in stray memory keys. One study, carried out in 2016 by Tischer and colleagues, was specifically focused on this question: why do people plug in thumb drives that they find lying around?

To answer this, the research team dropped 297 USB keys on a campus of the University of Illinois. They used a variety of different types of devices, with different labels, and dropped them at different locations on the campus, and at different times of the day. Each memory key contained files consistent with how they were externally labelled – however, every file was actually an Hypertext Markup Language (HTML) file that contained an <img> tag for an image located on a centrally controlled server. This allowed the researchers to detect when the file was opened, and also popped up a survey that explained the study and encouraged whoever had plugged in the device to answer some questions about why they had done so.

The authors report some eye-catching statistics. Checking the location of where the drives were dropped after a week, 290 of the 298 drives had disappeared. Of those, 135 (45 per cent) ended up being plugged in – hence the authors describe the attack's success as being in the 45–98 per cent range (though only 58 agreed to participate in the study).

In terms of motivation, a large majority of those who participated in the study said that they connected the drive simply in order to locate its owner (68 per cent). So, there, maybe, is your answer: people stick in stray USB keys because – being nice people – they want to get them back to their owners. To be blunt: your colleagues are going to plug in USB keys that they find lying around – no amount of scare messaging is going to stop them, so don't try. It is likely impossible, and indeed objectionable, to try to remove altruism from ordinary human beings via mandatory workplace training. Instead, why not try positively reinforcing a behaviour that you actually want them to do? So, continue dropping USB keys throughout your organisation, but make sure that you have a clear procedure of what you want users to do with them when they find them. Maybe you want them to take them to the IT desk, or to plug them into a designated, air-gapped machine – make sure they are rewarded as soon as they do.

Updates and anti-virus

In most organisations, issues such as software updates and anti-virus have been automated at a network level, so the results we received when we asked our survey respondents about them are perhaps understandable. As you can see from Table 5.2, these are things that many security professionals rarely or never focus on in training. However, it is still important that end users understand these processes and do not become complacent.

Don't forget, while you may be able to push out updates for most devices that your end users operate, that doesn't cover everything. Mobile security is an ongoing scary place where CISOs have less technical control than they would like. While 'bring your own device' (BYOD) practices may have reduced spending on IT equipment, they have markedly increased cybersecurity risk exposure. To be clear, these are risks that many organisations have decided to ignore, which is not a wise move at all. However, with subtle changes to organisational culture you can improve security behaviour, by simply spending a little bit of time nudging routines.

My advice here is to start small, with short coffee-break style standing meetings, where teams are encouraged to whip out their phones and compare operating systems. So, while Apple can push out security updates to iOS devices and generally badger users about installing them, users can still ignore these warnings. Security updates are even easier to ignore with Android devices. Arguably, end users will not deem this to be a security priority until it is made a business priority. Even with partitioned devices and advanced enterprise device management policies, essentially the user is the perimeter and should be treated as such. Get users' attention for as little as 15 minutes a month with their smartphones and simply get them to update their devices over a coffee. And that's it – making a little bit of time to get the end users to consciously engage with improving their cybersecurity behaviour.

Again, this feeds into workplace culture, which will be explored in the next two chapters, but it should also be seen as an important element of habitual behaviour. In other words, as a security professional, it is not enough that you encourage your colleagues to have anti-virus on, and always run the latest version of software by updating regularly. You must also advocate that employees are always given enough time in their workday to carry out these tasks too.

SUMMARY

In concluding this chapter let's summarise what we have learned about changing cybersecurity behaviour. To begin with, we started this chapter with a brief discussion of policy. If we want to change behaviour, it is important that this is specified in official policy, and that end users are aware of what is prohibited by policy. But more crucially, an atmosphere of fairness should be developed around cybersecurity, and end users should be part of the process of writing policy. If we are to positively influence behaviour, we must understand end users' perspectives on what works and what doesn't. This chapter also covered the relative effectiveness of those human behavioural tools known as punishment and reinforcement. In making the point that while the former seems to be far more popular in information security, the latter is preferred by behavioural scientists, we also considered the distinction between formal and informal reactions to violations of policies. Following this we moved on to explore strategies for changing specific cybersecurity behaviours and dealt with in turn access control, workstation locking, password management, anti-phishing, removable media and mobile security, and finally updates and anti-virus. In each of these cases, we evaluated peer-review research and best practice advice. Overall, readers are advised to start small, make changes gradually and foster an atmosphere of fairness and intellectual humility. Naturally, this feeds into workplace culture, which will be examined in Chapters 6 and 7.

NEXT STEPS

Let's wrap up with a few suggestions for where you might think about changing your colleagues' cybersecurity behaviours. Again, as with the last chapter, take baby steps with these interventions:

- Think about your own role. Are you leading by example with your own cybersecurity behaviour? Or is there anything you need to change?

- Additionally, how are you personally going to change behaviour within your organisation? What are the strengths and weaknesses of your position? Who do you need help from or buy-in from, before you even begin?

- What is the most effective method you can think of for making your colleagues more aware of your organisation's information security policy? And if it's not fair and equitable in its current state, how are you going to fix that?

- Think about how you will approach the two sides of the Dunning–Kruger effect with regard to claimed cybersecurity knowledge. How will you deal with these different types of people? How will you encourage an atmosphere of intellectual humility around cybersecurity behaviour?

- Using the 'positive reinforcement with chocolate' idea, plan out how you are going to change workstation lockout behaviour in your organisation. What is the best way of raising awareness of the 'muscle memory at loo break' method? Don't forget though about the complexity of measuring behaviours as described in Chapter 4!

- Consider what you will encourage end users to do with stray USB keys and how you will reward, rather than punish, this behaviour.

- Can you make it a company-wide policy to set aside a short timeslot for updating operating systems for smartphones and other mobile devices, whether iOS or Android?

6   UNDERSTANDING CULTURE

Bruce Hallas

Culture eats strategy for breakfast!

(attributed to Peter Drucker)

This is an old adage, widely used. It's often quoted when explaining some of the greatest failures in corporate history and international diplomacy. However, it is more often the unrecognised and therefore misunderstood root cause of many of the challenges we face, day to day, when trying to influence anyone to get behind a new or even old course of action including cybersecurity.

Mergers and acquisitions, often examined minutely by analysts and advisers, management consultants and the media and vastly experienced business and organisational leaders, have, at significant cost to stakeholders and society, failed to deliver against expectations. This is because building a culture was either not thought about or was treated as an afterthought following the decision to merge; or because it was assumed that the matter of integrating cultures was not a risk worth considering as part of due diligence; or that the challenges culture would pose would be ironed out through a change programme. These failures are often not because mergers and acquisitions didn't look great on paper, but because, in reality, data and information, on their own, don't make something a success. People make the possibilities that justify the merger and acquisition on paper a success in the long term, and people are both subject to, and influencers of, culture.

Now think about the investments made by governments and businesses in cybersecurity. It is estimated that in 2020 the global market for cybersecurity will amount to $173 billion. This, it is anticipated, will grow to $216 billion by 2023.[51] Much of this will be spent on engaging analysts, advisers, consultants and vendors of technical controls. The objective of much of this spend is to assess and define our appetite for risk and then to find and implement and review controls to manage that risk – including risky behaviours performed by people. These controls will include defining our organisation's expectations in terms of employee behaviour and culture. But will we learn from the mistakes made in the past when it comes to the role that culture plays in achieving success and our expectations?

Within the context of security those same forces are at work. What looks good on paper, in this case the organisational security policy, finds itself in the ring, facing off against the organisational culture. And there can only be one winner.

This chapter will explore the concept of organisational culture and some of the key factors that create and shape that culture. Organisational culture is a dynamic and ever-changing concept, driven by the people who work in an organisation, the interactions between them and the interactions between staff and the world outside the organisation. First, we'll define culture.

WHAT DO WE MEAN BY CULTURE AND ORGANISATIONAL CULTURE?

As innocuous a question as this might seem, it opens a can of worms. Definitions of culture can be found in any dictionary but those definitions can encompass a range of meanings and usages: just ask a microbiologist and a social scientist.[52] Unsurprisingly, there isn't a clear and, importantly, approved definition of the term organisational culture.[53] Without such a definition, our starting point for efforts to develop a security culture or to embed security into an organisation's culture is on shaky foundations. Without a clear definition of the term culture, or even awareness and behaviour, you introduce uncertainty. Uncertainty drives anxiety and stress. And, as I'll explain later, one, if not the main, purpose of culture is to reduce uncertainty and anxiety by introducing acceptable 'norms' and 'values', especially in some cultures around the world. These norms and values are an integral part of how behaviours are formed and influenced and tie closely with our decision- and judgement-making capacity as humans.

To draw an analogy, think of the potential for abuse of the risk assessment process. If such a process doesn't document, define and approve your risk decision criteria (the norms), at what point is your risk exposure unacceptable or acceptable? Suddenly the process of calculating your risk exposure is uncertain and can become driven by short-term factors, and is definitely subject to cognitive biases and heuristics that we all have. People make decisions that suit their needs, and when it looks like there's going to be too much work to do or the outcome doesn't fit their personal agenda, they make the easier decision instead of what might be best for all concerned.

A definition provides clarity about the objectives. You can either record the definition in the form of a sentence or paragraph or maybe even a range of bullet points. But the process of documenting this and obtaining agreement from all relevant stakeholders provides an anchor to which all decisions and actions can be tethered. Thus, a definition of culture provides clarity for the education and awareness manager who has been tasked with 'building a security culture' or 'embedding security into the organisational culture'. It provides the CISO, developing their team capacity and competency, with a clear sense of the roles, responsibilities and metrics of the team tasked with security awareness, behaviour and culture. And it provides options to address the long-standing challenge of how to measure metrics in a demonstrable and meaningful way.

The process of defining culture necessitates stakeholders agreeing, through a process of research and analysis, what 'culture' actually means to them.

Specifically, this process and a definition will provide the cybersecurity professional with an insight into the role culture plays in both forming and delivering the organisation's cybersecurity strategy. In my experience this process regularly highlights a fundamental flaw in how organisations tackle the challenge and leverage the opportunity of really considering culture. Is the Head of Education, Awareness and Culture responsible for creating a culture or leveraging an existing culture?[54] Does the 'security culture' actually belong to the security function? And if it does not, how can the security function actually be responsible for this? Does this mean that when we use the term 'responsible' what we are really allocating responsibility for is the process or facilitation of the process of embedding within the organisation's culture?

Most of us stumble at clearly defining the term culture. It is not uncommon, and arguably reasonable, to say that culture is intangible. This may explain why culture is often seen as an abstract concept. Its abstract nature is what, to many, makes the challenge of understanding, influencing and then measuring culture so difficult to overcome. Definitions of (organisational) culture include the following:[48]

- The accumulation of individuals' behaviours, goals and values.
- How employees think and act when management is not in the room.
- Culture is how things actually get done around here.
- Customs and rituals developed by a group over time.
- The norms and practices that organisations develop.
- The culture of a group is:

... a pattern of basic assumptions invented, discovered or developed by a given group as it learns to cope with its problems of external adaptation and internal integration that has worked well enough to be considered valid, and therefore, to be taught to new members as the correct way to perceive, think, and feel in relation to those problems.

(Schein, 1985, 2016)

- Culture is the social 'programming of the mind that distinguishes the members of one category of people from another' (Hofstede et al., 2010).
- Culture is behaviour and behaviour is culture (Hammerich and Lewis, 2013).

Even as we struggle to correctly define organisational culture, we have to contend with other factors that can influence and alter our perception and definitions of culture. We start looking at these factors by looking at the types of culture that have been identified.

TYPES OF CULTURE

Broadly speaking there are four categories of culture:

- macro-cultures: regional, national or religious;
- organisational cultures: any human-made organisational structure; organisational cultures are found in public, private and not-for-profit organisations;

- sub-cultures: occupational groups such as lawyers, doctors, accountants, teachers and cybersecurity professionals;
- micro-cultures: typically, social groupings of people around shared interests or common characteristics such as music, sport, hobbies and even age.

Macro-cultures

Many people, when they think of culture, consider this in the context of geographical regions, or countries, North America, Europe, South America, Middle and Far East, and Australia and New Zealand, or countries within these. The culture of these regions and countries is considered to be the prevalent values that drive and reflect normal behaviour within these societies. By normal behaviours we mean those behaviours the majority of individuals within a society find acceptable. The use of the term 'normal' illustrates that we recognise that these behaviours are not necessarily universally performed across society. After all, all societies experience those whose behaviours fall outside the cultural norms. The evidence of this surrounds us. You can most readily see this in the records of those who have appeared before court or who inhabit our prisons and other forms of detention, for example.

National cultures refer to beliefs, values and practices that are shared by the majority of people belonging to a nation, and enriched by national laws and governmental policies with respect to education, family life, business and other factors (Van Oudenhoven, 2001). A great deal of time and effort has been invested in 'profiling' national culture. There are several profiling frameworks that have been developed over time and the most commonly used framework is the work of Geert Hofstede and his son Gert Jan Hofstede.[49] In the 1980s Geert Hofstede performed research into the prevalent culture within IBM. This research has gone on to form the foundation of much of our understanding of culture from both a social and an organisational perspective. But it has also laid the foundation for Gert Jan Hofstede and fellow researchers, such as Michael Minkov, to further enhance this work in the past 40 or so years. In his research Hofstede listed what he called 'Dimensions of national culture' (see Table 6.1).

Table 6.1 Hofstede's dimensions of national culture[57]

Value	Description
Power distance index	This is a ratio that describes to what extent members within society are willing to accept unequal sharing or distribution of power. This value can be seen as a matter of hierarchy and a willingness of individuals to do as they are told by those in positions of authority.
Uncertainty avoidance	This describes how inclined a society is towards uncertainty or ambiguity. Uncertainty avoidance is sometimes referred to as a matter of truth. In a society with low tolerance for uncertainty there is one truth. In societies where there is a higher tolerance for uncertainty there may be more than one version of the truth.

(Continued)

Table 6.1 (Continued)

Value	Description
Masculine and feminine	In masculine societies there is a willingness to both use and to be subject to the use of force: the focus is on winning at all cost and often to the detriment of others; there's almost a cultural acceptance that only the 'fittest survive'. In feminine societies we see polar opposites to masculinity. This value is a way of thinking and being rather than a physical gender definition. Both women and men display characteristics that do not fall within their namesakes' value definition.
Long- and short-term orientation	This describes whether a society is indulgent and therefore focused on the short term, looking for the quick win, interested only in the present even where there's a great loss in its future from a given decision. A great example might be climate change. Or whether a society values and places a priority on the long-term view of what is good for itself and its members.
Individualism and collectivism index	Does society have more of a focus on what benefits the individual or what benefits the group or, more broadly, society. When we talk about success, are we talking about what's in it for me or what's in it for the group or society? Are we willing to change for the greater good even if it means giving something up ourselves that we value?
Indulgence and restraint index	This describes the tendency of a society to fulfil its desires. A high indulgence versus restraint score indicates that society encourages fulfilment of an individual's emotions and drives. A low score indicates the suppression of personal gratification, strict social norms and more regulation of people's behaviour and conduct.

According to Hofstede's research and backed up by further research over the last 40 years, nations can display a bias towards these values. While these descriptions are broad-brush, there is ready agreement that certain Western cultures display more masculine characteristics and certain Eastern cultures are more collective. While these values provide an opportunity to profile target audiences, they also materialise, day to day, in characteristics and attributes of given national cultures, in a more nuanced and often unrecognised way.

Often we can see these national values become tangible in the planning and delivery of advertising and other forms of marketing. For example, colours have different connotations and uses in different societies. In Japan a traditional wedding dress is likely to be red; funerals tend to be associated with the colour white. In many countries wedding dresses are traditionally white and funerals are closely associated with the colour black. The advertising of alcoholic drinks is not usually seen in Muslim countries, for obvious reasons.

Organisational culture

Organisational culture is often described as 'the way things get done around here'. If culture is the way things get done 'around here' then the process or everyday practices by which 'things get done' must be the 'organisational culture'.

Is there such a thing as organisational culture? The process of setting up an organisation and engaging people to support it in its mission will inevitably result in a culture evolving. The phrase 'start-up culture' is instantly recognisable. As the organisation evolves, its culture will naturally evolve with it to fit its environment. By environment I mean not just the physical or market environment but even the organisation's own stage in its evolutionary path. Start-up entrepreneurs, with one set of values, if successful evolve. Their growth requires scale, which often means attracting investment. But those investors have a different set of values at the heart of their decisions, and this affects the values at the core of the organisation. In turn people are recruited with similar values, and slowly the values of the organisation change and then permeate across the organisation's day-to-day processes. However, this evolutionary process within an organisation and the speed with which people change both within and outside the organisation can be outpaced by the speed of change in their business environment, the speed of change in technology or the speed of change in the social environment.

There may be smaller groups with specific tasks and in turn these groups may have macro-cultures. As such the term organisation could describe a group of people all working towards a stated goal or vision. Therefore, organisational culture may be an ideal way to describe the cultural context within which decisions are made day to day within an organisation.

Sub-cultures

Professions, such as doctors, lawyers, bankers and cybersecurity all have their own culture. Professional status is based on following a structured path of learning where individuals accumulate knowledge shared with them through formal educational processes, but also informally through work experiences and the groups, social media and other people we readily associate with day to day. Learning and working in these groups, combined with our natural behavioural bias towards social proof, means we look to others, especially when in new surroundings, to quickly establish the norms and acceptable behaviours. We assimilate the practices and behaviours associated with our profession or career path and identity. These processes for achieving and maintaining professional status, and the environment within which we use these skills, are common and relatively consistent across the world.

Micro-cultures

Micro-cultures are typically social groupings of people around shared interests or common characteristics such as music, sport or a sporting team, hobbies and even age. They are regarded as being more short-lived than other types of culture and may evolve or change much more quickly. In certain circumstances, these micro-cultures allow and encourage the relaxation of social norms (Fox, 2014). As micro-cultures involve shared interests, they may bring together differing age and social groups, resulting in the creation of different values and norms compared with the macro-cultures we have discussed (Arkalgud and Partridge, 2020).

Micro-cultures can be found in organisations in regional or branch offices, sales teams (compare inside versus outside or business to consumer (B2C) versus business to business (B2B) teams) and in the teams working on an assembly line. How these micro-cultures interact with each other and the cultures we have discussed above can play an important role in shaping both culture and culture change initiatives.

The process of developing a culture is more evolutionary in nature than we might expect. Initially people brought together will have a purpose in mind. This could be survival at the most basic level but would eventually move towards driving and maintaining economic or social prosperity or even self-actualisation as Maslow[58] would call it.

COMPONENTS OF CULTURE

Culture, within an organisation, is often considered abstract, yet many academics and people who perform culture change in organisations – not research (such as change management consultants and CISO), consider culture to have a structure. This structure is characterised by a mixture of abstract and intangible features as well as tangible ones. Edgar Schein's model,[59] sometimes termed the 'onion', set out three levels in an organisational culture:

1. Artefacts: structure and processes we can see, feel and hear. Heroes and symbols.

2. Espoused beliefs and values: statements made by organisational leadership usually in the form of aspirations, ideals and goals associated with beliefs in values recorded in documentation.

3. Underlying assumptions: unconscious assumptions made based on inherent values.

The first layer in the onion is 'artefacts'. These can range from office design, to the language used in conversations, to the way meetings are run and even dress codes. In the context of security, artefacts may include governance structure, organisational policy, processes and standards, by which either an organisation or the security function operates. You can think of these as your target operating model and should include governance, risk and control frameworks as a minimum. Heroes may be people with personal brands who are associated with security. They could include anyone in your security function with an outward facing role engaging across your organisation and even with external stakeholders. They can also include anyone, from across the organisation, who acts as an advocate for security, but doesn't work within the security function, such as security ambassadors, leadership and managers (or Jess's champions from previous chapters). Heroes definitely include those who have, through their own actions, chosen a path that has resulted in what I call a positive security outcome for the organisation and its stakeholders. But heroes don't and shouldn't always been seen as heroes in the context of security. Heroes, whether fictional or real, don't have to be heroes because of security. They can be heroes for any other reason so long as people look up to them or associate with them in a positive way.

The second level of Schein's onion is 'espoused beliefs and values', which are the aspirations of the organisation. They are usually identified and most definitely signed off by an organisation's senior leadership. They are commonly recorded in organisational statements that should, in theory, set out the organisation's 'true north'. However, anecdotally, in real life, away from the environment of the board and its senior management teams, there is often a difference or gap between what the board 'espouses' as being the organisation's beliefs and values and what those values actually are in practice. The same gap can be seen in how the board views daily operations and processes against what really happens day to day.[60] The existence of this gap fuels the sentiment that the board is detached from reality on the ground; it doesn't listen; or it ignores reality when it conflicts with perception. This serves to reinforce and entrench more deeply values at an operational level, which may actually cause excessive friction or lead to resistance when rolling out a new initiative (including a security strategy) and further reduce the trust relationship between employee and employer.

Individuals, who also have an important role to play in shaping organisational culture, will have their own values and their own view of how things should be done. How closely the values of the individual match the values of the organisation is very important, as individuals tend to resist change to their values and the imposition of values and procedures that clash with theirs. While individuals can work in situations where they experience a clash of values or thought, it can lead to cognitive dissonance[61] and a gap between what is said and what is done. Such gaps can damage an organisational culture and lead to the rise of sub-cultures. Individuals will also take cues from senior leaders; if a leader talks about 'compassion' and 'treating people fairly' as key values of their organisation and then fires people by text or email, then staff are just not going to believe the leader. The leader has demonstrated they don't believe in the values they espouse.

The final layer of the onion is 'underlying assumptions'. These are the outcomes of our unconscious or semi-conscious minds at work. Our judgement and decision-making faculty is much more based on unconscious thought than most of us would like to think or acknowledge. Advances in behavioural science have highlighted that, when it comes to making decisions, we're routinely less thorough than we think and we are driven consistently not by logic but by emotions influenced by the underlying, inherent assumptions prevalent within us. Our own underlying assumptions are brought into an organisation and combine with those of others to form an agreed set of underlying assumptions for the group. These assumptions include agreeing what 'truth' means, the importance of time, the ownership of space, the intrinsic aspects of human nature and how people should relate to each other.

These assumptions are deeply embedded within each and every one of us. The process of assimilating these values started from the day we were born and continues to the day when we face a choice between complying, or not, with our organisation's security policy. They are so well entrenched that changing them is notoriously difficult, but not impossible with sufficient and consistent investment of time and resources, as well as clear leadership from the board and across what Kotter (2012) would call a wide coalition of change stakeholders, over a prolonged period. With this in mind it is probably true to say that tactical initiatives, such as computer-based training, workshops, annual communication campaigns and induction days, on their own, are highly unlikely to bring about a change in culture. They may contribute to the journey, but on their own, much of the tactical quick fix solutions we see routinely marketed as driving cultural change tinker at the edges and don't go to the heart of the challenge.

> Many of the tactical quick fix solutions routinely marketed as driving cultural change tinker at the edges and fail to make any kind of cultural change.

We talked about culture in our introduction and we discussed a different model, created by Johnson and Scholes (see Johnson et al., 2012). Recapping, their model had six factors that influenced and made up organisational culture: stories and myths, rituals and routines, symbols, organisational structure, control systems and power structures. These six factors are very similar to many of the factors discussed by Schein and highlight that irrespective of how you look at culture, there are some basic components you ignore at your peril.

So while 'how things get done around here' may relate to artefacts and potentially espoused beliefs and values, where there is an element of compliance, the underlying assumptions, upon which day-to-day decisions are made, are actually the values at work influencing our judgement and decision-making capacity. Sometimes these are consciously driving decisions but, often, they are at work unconsciously, influencing outcomes day to day and minute to minute.

CULTURAL AWARENESS

In their book *Fish Can't See Water* (Hammerich and Lewis, 2013), the authors recognise that for almost all of us our own culture is invisible to us but that same culture can be observed by others from outside our culture. Our own awareness of our own culture is one of the first hurdles that those responsible for developing a security culture must recognise, understand and then accept if they are to effectively develop or embed an appropriate security culture into an organisation.

As a child I spent a considerable amount of time with my mother's family in the Mediterranean. I remember long summer holidays in glorious sunshine, a slower pace of life perfectly suited to the conditions we were surrounded by. Compare this with my life back home either in the UK or any other European country where my father was posted and there were notable differences. The challenges, problems and joys were all the same, but there was something different. The social norms were different. I still remember the first time I was asked to put on a swimming cap in Germany. It was something I had never had to do in the UK or in Malta. I remember the cycle paths of Germany and Holland, which were so different from the choices of cycling on a road in the UK or cycling on the path upsetting the pedestrians. It was these simple experiences that provided me with an awareness and appreciation for the differences that exist between people, and it is awareness of our own cultural biases and the environment that is the first step in developing our cultural context. So, how can we apply our insights to develop cultural context? Well, we start by being aware of the following:

- Culture is a force at play when you are trying to raise awareness and influence behaviour.
- You personally interpret the world around you through your own cultural lens.
- There is no right or wrong culture, just different interpretations of the same situation.
- Which cultures are at play and what the espoused and underlying assumptions are within these cultures.

If you aren't aware of the above then you need to start thinking about them and how you can apply them in your work. For awareness to have any meaningful effect you'll need to understand the 'why', which will help you reason with the need and place a value on its importance. Understanding the cultural 'why' or 'reasoning' soon helps to potentially explain the behaviours of those we seek to influence and often calls into question our labelling them as 'irrational' behaviours. They are only irrational because we can't explain them ourselves, to ourselves, and this more often than not is due to our own lack of awareness of the cultural context within which those decisions were made, as well as how people make judgements and decisions.

UNDERSTANDING THE CULTURAL FORCES AT PLAY

Having accepted the above it makes sense then to increase your own awareness of the cultural forces at play within the target audience. This invariably leads to organisational cultural surveys or the same thing by another name to try to avoid survey fatigue. Workshops are another option often used. But both have limitations. These all attempt to identify the underlying cultural attitudes towards information security, but rarely look at the overall values at work both in terms of the organisational culture and importantly the much broader and more deeply embedded national culture.

Often the design of these activities and their output is closer to a brand audit than a deep dive into the underlying culture or cultural attitudes towards security. A brand audit is important; however, it is not a complete assessment of the cultural forces at play, unless your definition of culture says it is so. There is, in many cases, a small crossover between a brand audit and cultural survey. Often the term 'brand' is misunderstood within the security industry. Many think of it as the 'identity', such as a logo associated with security. By brand we should actually mean: 'the overall experience by a customer that distinguishes an organisation or product from its rivals in the eyes of the customer'.

If when you read this you think, 'This sounds like marketing a product', then you're right, it does. That's because the similarities between the objective of raising awareness, influencing behaviour and fostering an appropriate culture around security and developing, marketing, selling and then providing customer service to your clients are fairly strong.

Brand audits do look at attitudes towards and maybe values associated with a particular brand. Cybersecurity is knowingly or unknowingly a brand both within an organisation and across the public. More often than not the current brand has evolved organically and the values that underpinned its success or growth to date aren't aligned or supportive of the prevailing organisational and national cultural values deeply embedded within the workforce. Where this happens, it can either cause a cultural clash between the values of security and those of the organisational culture or it can be aligned.

In national cultures where there is a tendency towards high uncertainty avoidance people might be more inclined to avoid the unknown. In cultures where there is a higher power to distance ratio people may be more inclined to do as they're told as long as they're actually told to do something and they're told to do this by someone who they respect or trust. In countries with a higher individualism and collectivism ratio we may expect the concept of 'What's in it for me', which appears to be a consistent principle in the design of education and awareness initiatives from Anglo-Saxon cultures. This may not suit audiences where what benefits the group and society is generally the culturally acceptable norm. As we've identified earlier (Table 6.1) there's even an indulgence and restraint index, with some countries scoring higher than others. Now how could this knowledge better help us to potentially design our efforts to influence behaviour and shape culture when it comes to security?

What are the cultural values that new employees or other third parties bring into any given organisation, which they've assimilated over many years? How can and will this affect your efforts to bring about changes in behaviour?

THE ROLE OF CULTURE IN DECISION-MAKING AND BEHAVIOUR

Outcomes is what it is all about. In some cultures those outcomes have to be measurable to have any meaning. In others they don't have to be measurable at all in the traditional metrics sense.

The outcome we desire from education and awareness activities is to:

- embed new behaviours;
- influence change to existing behaviours;
- reconfirm current acceptable behaviours.

We record the desired normal and acceptable security behaviours within policies, processes and procedures. These are the espoused values that we mentioned earlier and if these are complied with, knowingly or unknowingly, through choice or design, they result in the day-to-day practices and norms that make up some of the observable elements of culture.

But recording them doesn't make any difference to the behaviour of our audience unless we make them aware of these acceptable behaviours and they are also aware of them. While making someone aware, and that person being aware, may sound similar, there is a fine line between the two. One is the process for making someone aware of the acceptable norms and the other is the state of mind of the audience in terms of 'are they actually aware' what the acceptable norms are when they find themselves in a given situation, sometimes called situational awareness? In effect, do they actually consciously remember anything that you've made them aware of?

Memory retention is a metric I rarely see measured. The challenge of memory retention and recollection, which are again two different things, is a hurdle to be considered and overcome by those seeking to improve their chances of influencing behaviour where an organisation's definition of culture is restricted to normal acceptable behaviour outcomes. However, there is an exception to the need for conscious memory retention and recollection and that is unconscious retention and recollection leading to unconscious decision-making and behaviour. An alternative way of looking at this might be muscle memory or habit.[62]

Security controls, like almost every aspect of society, are designed on the assumption that if we make people aware of their roles and responsibilities, provide them with access to information or endless options, they will rationally weigh up the value, to them, between options, such as to comply or not comply. This is not the case in reality and is the reason why we often label employees as irrational when they make choices not to comply, when they know and understand the risks to themselves and others of non-compliance: your job is at risk, you will be disciplined, this could have an impact on customers and the organisation's bottom line. Some might think this was enough to influence or motivate employees to comply with policy. Anecdotally, most of us would recognise that such motivations do not work. And our anecdotal evidence and the gut instinct of many security professionals over the years is starting to materialise in the form of incident reporting data. For example, since the European Union General Data Protection Regulation was enacted in 2018, over 160,000 breach notifications have been reported.[63] This figure, on its own, arguably highlights the scale of the problem but also the lack of transparency, in the past, around data privacy and security and the difference between what is said in the form of policy statements, and what is done, day to day, on the ground by organisations when handling our personal data.

Humans are not creatures of logic. We do not weigh up the pros and cons of information and options nearly as well as we'd like to think. The evidence seems to be that any faith in our sense of logic is flattery, if not negligent, especially in circumstances where we are ill-informed or incorrectly informed, where we have no immediate feedback or where we are under some external pressure to make a decision quickly.

Our understanding of how people make judgements and decisions has advanced rapidly over the past 30 years. These advances have challenged the assumption that humans are logical and that the brain acts as a rational, mathematical processor of information.[64]

In 2002 Daniel Kahneman won the Nobel Prize for Economics for his work delivering 'integrated insights from psychological research into economic science, especially concerning human judgment and decision-making under uncertainty'. Since then Richard Thaler has also won a Nobel Prize for similar work.[65] Kahneman and Thaler built their work on the shoulders of many before them, and between them they have developed academic disciplines such as behavioural science and behavioural economics.

In brief, this work, along with other research, provided data that illustrated the case that human beings have two decision-making pathways:[66] a fast, intuitive and effortless pathway (System 1) and a slower, deliberative and logical pathway (System 2). We tend to use System 1 in our day-to-day lives and it is this system that uses heuristics and biases to reach a quick decision. Heuristics are the 'rules of thumb' or shortcuts, based on previous experience or knowledge that we apply as part of our decision-making process.

Heuristics have both evolutionary and learned aspects. For example, the affect heuristic, where we make decisions based on how we feel emotionally about them – 'trusting your gut instinct', for example – likely has a deep evolutionary history and is in evidence in other species (Kralik et al., 2012). But in specific contexts, such as when attempting to change your organisation's cybersecurity culture, we may encounter individuals who have learned to apply heuristics to their particular workload. For example, take the effort heuristic, where we place higher value on things into which we have put more time and energy (Kruger et al., 2004). Perhaps this is a phenomenon that you can see within the organisations you work with, where employees love the projects they have worked hard on, but not the ones they didn't have to put any effort into. But these heuristics – and others – can be irrelevant and bias our decisions. System 2 requires effort to use; it is the 'thinking hard' pathway. As such, we tend not to engage System 2 if we are under pressure, stress or we think we already know the answer.[67]

Remembering that culture relies on behaviours and that behaviours can be driven by our own decisions on what to do in a particular situation, we can now start to link these important ideas together. Many people in an organisation will have experienced and learned a number of acceptable or required behaviours, a number of heuristics (shortcuts) and biases from working in their team, function or group. When they are confronted with a decision to be made in the workplace, especially if they are under time or other pressure, System 1 will kick in. Processes or activities requiring 'hard thinking' – System 2 – will, in all likelihood, not be followed. When we think about many of the activities linked to cybersecurity, they will require the use of System 2 thinking for most non-specialists, because those non-specialists do not have the same heuristics and frames of reference as we security professionals do. So, when faced with a cybersecurity decision, most people (non-specialists) will follow the behaviours other people demonstrate (an illustration of the power of social proof[68]) or use a System 1 decision-making approach. Thus the culture becomes self-reinforcing; people do what they see other people doing and then it becomes part of their in-built decision-making process.

Culture as a point of vulnerability as well as strength

If culture is made of espoused values, practices and underlying assumptions common to any given group, whether national, organisational or even professional, and these have a significant impact on the choices people make, then can they be a point of vulnerability as well as a strength (see Kemp, 2004)?

A mature approach to cybersecurity includes identifying and assessing vulnerabilities within people, processes and technology and understanding what, if any, threats could exploit these, the impact should this happen and the likelihood of the threat materialising. If culture is part of our mental programming, as argued by social anthropologists, and is a powerful unconscious influence on the decisions we make, then this knowledge could arguably be used to design attacks against organisations, resulting in a compromise of data security and privacy.

This argument then forces us to consider whether we should include culture as a threat or vulnerability to our organisation and include it in our risk assessment methodology and in our risk assessments. If we as cybersecurity professionals clearly identify culture as a risk, then we will need to be able to present quantitative or qualitative measures of its impact on the business and on the controls we implement.

THE ROLE OF CULTURE IN 'AWARENESS'

As we will go on to discuss later, cultures are formed under the influence of many stakeholders. Formal structures exist that are both part of culture and responsible for embedding culture into the members of a group, whether they are working within an organisation or living within a nation state. Education, at all levels, from nursery through to professional training, is an example of a formal structure.

Informal structures predominately focus on the day-to-day living experiences of individuals: what they see, feel and hear in the environment in which they live or work and how others within their group respond to those environments. In the work environment, individuals become aware through experience of everyday practices of how things get done, including the shortcuts taken or the failure to comply with the organisation's policies and processes.

In the work environment, employees, especially new ones, mirror the behaviours they become aware of around them. In behavioural science it is well documented that people are subject to cognitive biases and heuristics, one of which is called social proof. People, more often than they would like to admit, are heavily influenced by other people's behaviours on an unconscious level. This is only natural as people prefer to identify with a group. They mirror behaviours as part of a survival instinct, herding, and because they do not want to be seen to stand out. This mirroring behaviour is common especially in environments or in relation to things that the individual doesn't know much about or where the environment is new to the individual. This is even the case where people have been made aware of the rules, have gone through formal education, have demonstrated competency around the rules and their roles and responsibilities and have witnessed or experienced the impact when things go wrong. A good example of this is cultural attitudes towards driving.

In many ways if we could crack the organisational culture, then this alone would drive levels of ongoing awareness, as the culture would demonstrate the behaviours we wish to be followed from a security perspective.

HOW ARE CULTURES LEARNED?

If your job title or role is to bring about change in an organisation's culture, whether that's introducing a new set of values, leveraging existing ones or looking to scale back others, then it seems natural that understanding how cultures are formed and influenced is going to be of some help.

In our enthusiasm to bring about change, do good and be seen to be making early progress, especially against our goals, it's tempting to launch straight into tactical initiatives to bring about a security culture.

We often label these 'quick wins' or 'low-hanging fruit'. These initiatives should be welcomed, so long as they contribute to the longer-term vision and don't undermine the foundations that need to be put in place. However, their effectiveness at bringing about cultural change is arguably limited.

From the moment we're born we start experiencing life through our senses and interpreting this using our brain. Now our senses aren't fully operational at this point and neither has our brain developed its full capacity. However, humans have evolved so that both our senses and our brain are sufficient at the point of birth to be able to do what they need to do, which is survive.

However, a newborn can't survive on its own. It is reliant on others to survive. Maslow's theory provides an interesting sense of the parents' initial role of provider of food, physical safety, warmth and so on. Initially this is the parents' role and it is here, as this small group, where we start to experience the importance of belonging to a group and become reliant on the impact of group dynamics.

Our brains and senses are well on the way to developing the capacities we often take for granted. But some senses are more developed and effective than others. All of this combined means our experiences of life are becoming broader and richer in terms of both content and emotion. The process of learning the acceptable norms within our group continues to evolve.

As we develop, from a newborn to a toddler and then move into early education, it is generally true within many cultures that the group within which we experience and become aware of the acceptable norms tends to get bigger.

When we start our early education, away from our close and extended family as well as their friends, we enter into a formal structure for learning. That learning is both structured and informal. Meeting other children and adults introduces us to their values. Where their values are similar or the same, they reinforce our own values. It also introduces us via the education system to policy and espoused values of key stakeholders, beyond our family and friends, including government, for example. The increasing role of government, through education as well as several other policy areas, means the institutions who we entrust with our children are significant players in embedding culture and cultural values into our children.

As children get older the role of formal and informal structures in their development continues. Their experience of applying cultural norms increases and their day-to-day encounters of life escalate. They branch out and pursue interests, establish groups of friends with similar interests and develop a shared experience of those interests with others within their social groups.

It's not unusual at this stage to find children stepping out and finding their own two feet. Their relationship and reliance on the traditional family and extended family and friends' connections will potentially change, especially in some cultures.

At this stage in life and the education system many people start to focus, whether of their own volition or because of an external factor, on a particular path for developing skills. Children are asked to think about their future profession, career or some other means of making a living and contributing to society.

Those choices appear to be discretionary. However, there are forces already at play stacking the odds in one direction or another. Family, friends, media and school all have an influence. When choices are made we commit to a particular course of action and sometimes study. Our circle of day-to-day contacts changes and we enter another period of the development of our cultural compass as we experience what it means and takes to pursue a particular career or skills set.

At a basic level many of these careers and skills are common across industries and national boundaries. Most professions have a relatively consistent structure, process, procedures and standards for achieving professional status in any country. Often these are accompanied by shared values and experiences as well as myths, rituals and stories. This applies just as much to those career and life choices that do not fall under what we traditionally think of as 'professions'.

Then we find employment or work, within organisations or for ourselves, and join the workforce. The organisations we join in many ways are micro systems living and operating within a much greater system.

It is within these organisations we believe that we experience 'organisational culture' for the first time and, in many ways, the literature and industry thinking reflects this. However, there's also a clear, undeniable argument that we have already experienced organisational culture through our participation in the education system, membership of social, sporting or other similar groups and our experience of family and life up to the date when we start working within organisations. These organisations of people don't take the immediate form of organisations we work within, as employees, suppliers or some other form; however, they are organisations in almost every aspect.

We are exposed to organisational cultures from the moment we are born through our families, education, hobbies, friends and work. Organisational culture is not something we experience for the first time when we join the workforce.

Forming organisational culture

Is how organisational cultures are formed any different from the explanation about how national culture is formed? In many respects I don't think so. But with two simple exceptions.

First there is the matter of choice. We have no choice in the matter when it comes to our own birth, where we are born, who our family is and the process by which we grow and develop, especially in our early years.

Second, when we are born most would argue that we turn up with a metaphorical 'clean sheet' as far as culture goes. As a newborn, we have not experienced cultural programming through life experiences but, as we grow, those experiences, both formal and informal, and our awareness of these, means we start to assimilate the culture in which we grow. This might explain how in the second and subsequent generations of migrants, original cultural values change over time. This may further explain the intergenerational gaps that are fostered as the younger generation assimilates the cultural values of a host country through their life experiences and interaction within their host nations or group's members.

However, on a relatively simple level the similarities between how organisational and national cultures are formed are quite clear. Table 6.2 presents some examples.

Table 6.2 Common factors influencing the creation of national and organisational cultures

Outside the workplace	Within the workplace
Parents	Organisation founders/leadership.
Family	Leaders/managers/department.
Informal education	Day-to-day experience, sharing and observing of 'how things are done around here' or the values, practices and characteristics that are recognised and rewarded or penalised.
Formal education	Structured learning and development within an organisation on its espoused values and artefacts or professional development around skills. Assessing knowledge and competency of all of these.
Friends	Work colleagues you engage with closely day to day. Peers. Almost friends within a work context, possibly people you'd actively meet outside work because you have a shared interest.
People you interact with	Work colleagues you interact with but strictly in a work scenario.
	Other people whom you may or may not see or know at work or with whom you might engage due to work, such as customers/suppliers or other external stakeholders.
Media including all external stakeholders who develop and distribute content	Internal communication activities.
Social media	Social media.

Organisational culture: top down or bottom up?

Unsurprisingly, there is much debate about whether culture can be formed or changed from the top or the bottom of an organisation. Proponents of the 'top down' model make the not unreasonable assumption that if senior management (or their boss) says something is important – and changes their behaviour to match – then it is something they should follow. This calls up the idea of leaders and artefacts as mechanisms to change or influence culture.[69] The same can also be said of cultures in start-ups; as these organisations are typically small, the influence and visible practices (rituals and routines) of the founder-leaders define and shape the culture going forward.[70] Interestingly, the UK financial regulator (termed the Financial Conduct Authority (FCA) at the time of writing) suggested that 'culture comes from the past',[71] as 'mindsets are developed and reinforced over years and even decades and are passed down from one generation to the next'. We could thus state that culture is not necessarily changed from the top down but could be reinforced top down.

Another view is that organisational culture develops daily as a result of the interactions between staff, staff and customers, staff and competitor employees and so on. The sum total of these interactions drives and shapes the corporate culture and, by changing how the majority of individuals carry out their work and their behaviours, changes the culture. These changes are then perceived by senior management, who act to capture and confirm the changes they see as being of benefit.[72]

However, I suspect there may be a third way, just as in the setting and execution of organisational strategy: 'middle out'. In this model, it is the decisions and judgements of middle managers who typically link lofty strategic goals to the day-to-day reality that determine the success, failure and overall implementation of the strategy. Likewise, how these individuals interpret the cultural messaging from senior management and apply that in the context of their teams, business targets and business environments will influence how the culture changes.

HOW ARE CULTURES INFLUENCED?

The answer to this question varies depending on how you interpret the term culture.

If you take a behaviouralist focus where culture and behaviour are one and the same, then your approach will be focused on influencing behaviour.

Behaviour is covered elsewhere in this book; however, it can be influenced in several ways: we can attempt to influence a single behaviour; influence multiple behaviours; use a single tool or intervention to drive change; or we can use multiple tools to drive change. But at a simple level we can design working environments that give people no option but to do it our way, using technical or process interventions. We can also design working environments where certain choices are rewarded, or promoted, or made easier than other choices, using what is termed choice architecture. Choice architecture refers to the practice of influencing choice by 'organising the context in which people make decisions', or 'choice architecture can be used to help nudge people to make better choices (as judged by themselves) without forcing certain outcomes upon anyone'.[73] The design, layout and functionality of workspaces, cafeteria and software can be altered or include choice architecture from the beginning to change the context in which people make decisions. We discussed earlier the impact of moving fruit and chocolate around in a shop. In the work environment we can influence behaviour by building processes that require a security step or integrate security, so that individuals have no choice but to perform a task in a secure manner,[74] or we can make certain choices difficult to pursue by requiring reporting, bureaucracy and time for completion. We can attempt to influence behaviours, by making people aware of our expectations and educating them so they are competent to fulfil these expectations and choose to do so when confronted with a given situation. We can understand how behaviours are formed and influenced and the role of culture within this and then use these principles to drive whatever change initiative we put in place.

Using choice architecture is considered a more interventionist approach. Such an approach reduces the human factor and associated risk from the equation along with the choices made when identifying, approving, implementing and managing the actual architecture. The approval process for investing in such a choice architecture, if it can be traced all the way to the top, may be interpreted as demonstrating a board culture where security is valued. If we use choice architecture and design it correctly, we do not remove choice from our employees: we make the desired choice an easier choice to make. In other words, choice architecture stacks the odds in our favour of a positive security behaviour and outcome. The choice architecture doesn't guarantee that the desired choice will be made and, therefore, you can argue that where the employee still chooses a course of action, they are making a positive choice.

However, removing the option from employees to make a positive security choice by using interventions, such as technical controls that block actions, or the design of processes that give you only one way to get things done are behavioural interventions, rather than choice interventions. If we deliberately curtail choice, do we actually minimise the move towards fostering an organisational culture where security is truly valued by everyone? If employees don't have to think for themselves when it comes to security, if employees become ambivalent to it, are they culturally aware or contributing to the security culture in a positive manner?

Some may interpret implementing choice architecture as somewhat Machiavellian, manipulative and an erosion of trust between employer and employee. Others may see them as interventions that go too far and bring them directly into conflict with values and underlying assumptions. Examples can include a technical control that enforces a policy no matter how hard you try to break it being used in an organisation where individual freedom, thought and action are part of the underlying values. The control will be seen as reducing the 'rights' of individuals to do things their way. Or turn gates at the office reception that only allow one person through at a time and don't allow you to pass your office swipe card back to someone waiting on the other side, where an underlying value is to help out people in trouble.

If you take a broader view that culture is about the values that drive choices, which result in observable behaviour, and which underline the elements that make up both national and organisational culture, then your approach will probably incorporate a wider view of the challenge other than behavioural intervention and choice architecture. In an organisation, building a culture that aligns both organisational values and individual values[75] and linking strategy to culture are seen as key determinants[76] to building, strengthening and influencing culture. The penalties for ignoring culture or value alignment, or promoting poor cultural norms are regularly exposed these days.[77]

Building on the observation that national and organisational cultures are formed as an output of formal and informal structures and experiences, as detailed in this chapter, then it stands to reason that they can also be influenced by them.

That means culture is both flexible and dynamic, responding to changes in the environment that both nurtures and hosts it as well as benefits from it. This should give all of us responsible for embedding values and practices associated with security into organisations and society a degree of optimism. Some of these changes, specifically any change in values, can take a long time to take shape and others can appear to materialise relatively quickly. It's not unusual to see internal communication campaigns, which can be rolled out within a year or less, extolling the organisation's espoused values when it comes to security. However, just because you invest in a communications campaign to share those values it doesn't make the underlying assumptions or values change.

In this chapter we have considered culture within the context of society as a whole as well as culture within the context of an organisation. The emphasis has been on how cultures are formed at a national and an organisational level. By understanding these formal and informal influences on culture we can identify the wide range of opportunities to intervene and shape an organisation's, or even society's, cultural attitude towards security as shown in Table 6.3.

Table 6.3 Major factors that influence culture

National or organisational culture	Levels or manifestations of culture	Description/example	Questions to ask yourself
National	Values	Prevailing cultural values amongst your target audience for change.	What are the values the audience talk about? What is considered 'right' or 'wrong'? How can these be leveraged in how you design your current and future change programme or efforts?
National	Practices	These practices can be formal, such as legislation, regulation or membership of groups of people.	How can these be leveraged? How could these practices impact your programme?

(Continued)

Table 6.3 (Continued)

National or organisational culture	Levels or manifestations of culture	Description/example	Questions to ask yourself
National	Rituals	The rituals existing in society that individuals experience as part of a group.	Can I capture the rituals? What part of the ritual is key to joining or staying in a group?
		Interactions between individuals.	How can these be leveraged?
		Induction to an organisation, professional body or sports team are examples of a ritual.	How could these rituals impact your programme?
National	Heroes	Heroes and influencers amongst the audience.	Can I meet or use these heroes?
		Heroes associated with values, attributes or characteristics associated with security.	What do they embody (values, attributes, behaviours)?
			How can these be leveraged?
			How could these heroes impact your programme?
National	Symbols	Visual identities associated with security (such as 'stop signs' or 'warning' symbols).	What is the imagery? How is that imagery perceived?
			Is security seen as a positive or negative?
			How can these be leveraged?
			How could these symbols impact your programme?
Organisational	Artefacts	These include an organisation structure, records, processes, visible behaviours, rituals, buildings within which the organisation is based and even an organisations brand and the story it tells.	Where in the organisations structure is the responsibility for security lie?
			What policies, processes and procedures are in place?

(Continued)

Table 6.3 (Continued)

National or organisational culture	Levels or manifestations of culture	Description/example	Questions to ask yourself
Organisational	Espoused values	Organisations values as stated in policies, contracts, and rules. Written values of the security function. Alignment between functions, groups and teams and alignment across the organisation.	Start with understanding gap between what is said are the organisations values and what are the actual organisational values. Can security values be aligned or do they come into conflict?
Organisational	Underlying assumptions	Actual day to day assumptions within the organisation. Day to day perceived and actual values associated with security. Underlying values of the work force which they brought with them before working for an organisation.	What actually happens? Where and how does the actual diverge from the espoused (written) values? What cultural influences or cultures are there in the organisation's environment? How can these divergences be leveraged? How could these assumptions impact your programme?

The table highlights what we consider to be the major factors that influence culture. We highlight the fact that a number of the manifestations of culture listed here (heroes, behaviours) have been discussed by other authors in this book and reinforce the tight linkage between awareness, behaviour and culture.

WHY IS CULTURE OF INTEREST IN A SECURITY CONTEXT?

Other than the lack of understanding of what we mean by the term 'culture', there is I believe a difference of opinion about why culture is of interest. When we think about the organisations we work in, we can now see there are at least three cultures we may wish to examine: the overall organisational culture, the security culture and the culture of the security function.

So, when we say 'security culture' are we:

- laying down an objective to develop a security culture within an organisation?
- referring to the current security culture within an organisation?
- saying that we must understand the role of culture in achieving our end goals as professionals working within the security context?
- examining the culture of the security professionals and function?

So, when we think about culture, where are we aiming? Why are we interested? Do we think that by changing 'the culture' we will see better security outcomes, less incidents and a happier, more educated workforce? Importantly, why should non-security individuals be interested?

SUMMARY

Culture is not as simple as it first seems. While we all know it when we see it, it's much more difficult to reduce to an easy-to-grasp definition we can all agree on. In part, that's because culture is made of tangible and intangible components; we can easily see the tangible but may struggle to identify the intangible. As the reader is aware, the intangible can often be the major force in shaping the culture we observe. Again, while we all know culture can change, it's subject to many influences, so finding the influences with the most impact and ability to cause lasting change can also be difficult. We've briefly looked at differing types of culture, from the national to the team, from the organisational to the professional. It is true that many of these types of cultures display the same characteristics and influences; furthermore, each cultural type interacts with other cultural types, so we can see that culture is a rich tapestry.

Finally, we've discussed how we can approach culture change from a behaviouralist perspective, invoking the concept of choice architecture, and from a values perspective.

We will now use our understanding of culture as the launchpad to examine how we can change culture in the next chapter.

NEXT STEPS

Aside from reading one or more of the books we've quoted to gain a deeper insight into the topic, we would recommend that you take a very practical approach:

- Answer the questions presented in Table 6.3 – identify the elements that make up your organisational culture.
- Sharpen your focus and identify the organisational security culture.
- Describe the culture of the security function or team using a cultural model.

7　CREATING CULTURE

Bruce Hallas

In the previous chapter I explained how culture is understood, generally and in an organisational context. This chapter summarises how, having understood how cultures are formed, we may use this to start to build a cohesive approach to embedding cybersecurity values into organisations, industry sectors and even, arguably, nation states, through a cybersecurity culture.

For many of this book's readers their role will be to bring about a change in culture within an organisation or to 'develop a security culture'. The scale of this journey is, as you will anticipate, large, so this chapter is not a definitive guide, nor is it a checklist to take to your CISO or board. It is, however, a small but influential part of the ABC journey to help enable you to take a confident step forward on this most critical of tasks.[78]

In the previous chapter we mentioned the mantra that culture comes from the top down. I explained an alternative, and complementary, view to this, where culture came from every direction. There are plenty of examples of cultural values at work where the leadership of an organisation is not present or, in some cases, is the target of employee displeasure about the cultural gap between what the employees understood to be the organisation's values, and what the leadership are describing them to be. These, on their own, illustrate the need to see culture more broadly than just a 'top down' challenge.

> The 'top down approach' is widely accepted by many commentators, especially those commentators from Western cultures or those familiar with Western management styles or theories. I think it's only fair to say that some readers of this book, with different cultural values, may disagree entirely or partially with this assumption. And, as someone who has taken the time to research 'culture' without the 'cybersecurity' overhead, I'm entitled to agree.

Organisations and their leadership are, on the whole, reluctant investors in cybersecurity. In the ideal world there wouldn't be a need to invest in security. However, the world isn't ideal and it is, I'm happy to say, full of people.

As an observation, based on my own 20+ years' experience working within the industry, the biggest drivers of investment and change appear to have been: suffering from an incident, statutory obligations, regulatory obligations and supply chain pressure.

When it comes to engaging a new supplier or going through the process of contract renewal, we're seeing a small but growing trend for supplier organisations to provide assurance that they have in place an education and awareness strategy or plan. Some contracts seek assurances about security culture specifically. This is something your client-facing CISO and legal counsel are most likely to come across. In my experience most of these requests for assurances related to contracts or suppliers working in regulated industries such as finance and insurance. However, with legislators and regulators increasingly upping their game I forecast that we will see a rise in requests for such assurance. This will focus attention across organisations on answering this in a meaningful and demonstrable way, just as ISO/IEC 27001, NIST, GDPR and other trends within supplier management have done in the past.

CAN CULTURES BE CREATED?

The question of whether a culture can be created is really irrelevant. This is because the nature of humanity means that the mere existence of a group of people, that is two or more people living or working together, means that they will develop a set of acceptable norms, and values that underpin these, for how they behave and interact between themselves. This is culture.

A better or more helpful question is, 'should I create a "security culture" or can I create a security culture within an existing culture, such as within an organisation?'

The phrase security culture could be interpreted as a culture separate and distinct from another culture. Is this actually helpful when engaging with stakeholders across the organisation? Is this what we actually mean when we use the phrase 'security culture'? Or are we actually talking about embedding security into an organisation's, or even across a society's, day-to-day culture?

Again, the answer to the last question is likely to be, yes, we are talking about embedding security into an organisation's culture: in fact a culture will already exist. Whether this culture was planned or has evolved organically and not on an agreed and desirable path is another question entirely. The organisation's founders and leaders will instil their values and practices. Those values, behaviours and the culture that succeed and enable the organisation to survive and then grow will become recognised as the acceptable practices and norms. New employees will bring with them their own cultural attitudes and perceptions towards security from their previous experience.[79]

Bearing in mind the above, for many the question is not whether a culture can be created but rather whether the existing culture can be changed.

CAN CULTURE CHANGE?

Again, the answer is yes. If culture is formed through the processes outlined in this chapter then changes in those processes will naturally result in a change of culture. Culture is dynamic and is shaped by the forces at work in the environment within which any group of people live, work and play.

But change at a cultural level is a significant investment of resources. Change in any context requires organisations to go through the stages outlined in Table 7.1, according to Kotter.[80]

Table 7.1 Kotter's stages for change

Kotter's stages for change	Description	Points to consider
Urgency	Make this a priority. A top priority.	If it's a 'good idea' then it's just an idea.
		What is the imperative behind the need for change?
		Does everyone know and understand the reasons why?
		Does everyone know and understand their role?
		Does everyone know, understand and accept how they will be measured personally?
Powerful coalition	Appropriate stakeholders with authority to authorise, support and enable change.	What are the terms of reference behind your cultural change programme?
		Who are the stakeholders?
		Is it a broad range of the organisation's stakeholders or is there a bias towards security and at best HR, learning and development (L&D)?
A vision	What is the end state? What will success look and feel like?	Leaders give vision.
		Management deliver on this. Where is your vision for a security culture coming from?
Communication	Clear and effective processes for two-way communication.	Communication is vital. But communication for communication's sake can be counterproductive.

(Continued)

Table 7.1 (Continued)

Kotter's stages for change	Description	Points to consider
Authority	There must be authority to approve and enable change invested in stakeholders. Or the stakeholders must have qualities that give them natural authority usually associated with leadership.	Who has the authority to push barriers aside to make progress? What's the process for doing this?
Success stories	Identify and communicate early success stories to build momentum.	What does success actually mean and how will you be able to demonstrate it in a clear and meaningful way?
Consolidating	Build on early success and maintain ongoing and greater momentum.	Does success sometimes drive complacency about the rest of the change programme?
Anchoring into the existing culture	Embed into everyday practices.	What are the opportunities for drilling the culture into the day to day fabric of your organisation?

I would add to Kotter's well-recognised process that the precursor to the stages in Table 7.1 is to understand how behaviours are formed and influenced. After all, effective change is about understanding the human factor and designing your change programme with that understanding in mind.

WHY CHANGE CULTURE?

Given that changing culture seems to be a difficult process, why would a CEO, a manager or even the security professional attempt to change it? There are many reasons but we can group them into three categories, discussed below.

External factors (compliance and precedence)

Governments and industry regulators are a key driver of change in terms of the time and effort organisational leaders pay to information security and risk management.

Governments prefer stability within which economies and societies tend to, historically, grow more effectively. This growth and stability historically has kept the majority of the population happy and the status quo has been maintained. This in turn means those in power retain this power, especially in cultures with a greater power distance ratio, between those at the bottom and those in power at the top.

Laws and regulations are much like organisational policies. They are tools governments use to intervene and drive perceived stability around agreed acceptable norms. They may not always be used effectively; however, they are part of the government's arsenal to intervene to embed policy. In organisational culture these would be espoused values.

Increasingly we are seeing these tools stipulate the need for organisations to implement a security culture. Possibly of greatest impact, we often see through the media and legal review that regulators and the courts are pointing the finger of blame at CEOs and the board for creating or enabling an environment where negative cultural attitudes within an organisation towards cybersecurity or privacy were allowed to foster. And that this is the root cause behind yet another breach and not the failure to update a piece of software. This lack of an appropriate culture is then the backdrop for calculating the penalty or fine handed to the CEO and other stakeholders. And those fines are getting bigger. And the damage to the individuals' reputation is getting larger and becoming difficult to move on from in some cases.

Thus, we see culture change initiatives being driven from the top down, as senior managers mandate changes in processes and routines to enhance compliance. Another reason for adopting this top down approach, at least for organisations with a general Western cultural emphasis, is that regulators increasingly point to 'toxic culture',[81] a 'lack of culture' or something similar, from the top, as the reason or root cause behind some of the biggest data security breaches we see reported in the media.

We can see how governments and regulators are starting to view culture and its influence in organisations by looking at the UK FCA and its views. We've already come across some of its views on organisational culture in the previous chapter; now let's examine its views on security culture. The FCA[82] has stated:

> We expect 'a security culture', driven from the top down – from the Board, to senior management, down to every employee. This is not as vague as it sounds – I will elaborate further.

> We are looking for firms to have good governance around cybersecurity in their firms – by this I mean senior management engagement, responsibility – and effective challenge at the Board.

> We are aware firms have found it difficult to identify the right people for these roles – but much progress has been made, and I am encouraged by the engagement we have seen on this issue by senior management.

While the FCA's guidance here is helpful, it does highlight shortcomings in terms of defining how to comply with any requirement for an appropriate 'security culture'; governance, or espoused values as cultural specialists would call it, is not all that makes up 'culture', as we have discussed previously. The FCA's interpretation of what culture means, or how it can be evidenced, in itself shows a limited understanding of how cultures are formed and influenced. This may play well into the hands of those who see culture as a tick-box exercise rather than a means to drive changes in risk stemming from employee or other stakeholder behaviour.

As a further indication of how regulators view culture, the Monetary Authority of Singapore (MAS, 2020) has published its *Information Paper on Culture and Conduct Practices of Financial Institutions*, in which it states:

> Culture is generally understood as the shared values, attitudes, behaviour and norms in an organisation. It is driven by both the 'hardware' (e.g. policies and processes) and 'software' (e.g. beliefs and values) in an organisation.

MAS also places a requirement on senior management to 'walk the talk' and appoint culture and conduct champions. The top down approach must be met by an 'echo from the bottom' with rewards for employees seen to be embodying the culture in their work. Finally, the paper states that:

> The various components contributing to the culture and conduct of an organisation do not work in isolation. They are inter-related and can help to complement and reinforce each other.

– a point that we heartily echo.

I would also re-emphasise here the increasingly clear message, from regulators in their industry engagement and education roles, for organisations to demonstrate an appropriate organisational culture when it comes to cybersecurity and what this might mean. Regulators need to understand that the words they use can either create a rod for the back of security professionals and drive a compliance culture or, if done properly, can equip stakeholders responsible for delivering cultural change with meaningful leverage via legislation, precedent and education.

Here I raise a word of warning. The CISOs, and education and awareness managers I work with understand the value of drawing on regulator commentary and findings from investigations. This helps them set out clear objectives when it comes to culture strategy. However, time is against you if your strategy is based on what others say instead of developing your own vision. Let me explain.

When a regulator, judge or even customer, comments on their understanding of the term 'culture', it must be remembered that it was at a single point in time. Regulators', judges' and customers' interpretation of the term 'culture' is likely to change. This change is a result of them becoming more aware, educated and knowledgeable on how cultures are formed and influenced. Sometimes this will be as a result of their own research and sometimes as a result of what the collective understanding is, among the groups and cultural institutions within which they live out their lives. Why is this important?

If you use only these terms and definitions, comments and precedents as the guiding principles behind a new culture strategy, and let us say, for argument's sake, that the desired culture change takes three to five years to implement, then it is quite likely that the regulators' interpretation of culture will have changed. Basically, if your strategy for cultural change is based around delivering against what regulators say now, then you are setting yourself up to fail in three years' time.

> An effective strategy for change is about delivering where you need to be in the future, not where you should be now!

We should recognise that there are many other external factors apart from compliance and precedence, such as the competitive environment, sales performance, competitor and consumer behaviour, and national and sub-culture values that can influence our culture, our values and our behaviours.

Internal factors

A new CEO; a change of strategy; a 'burning platform'; an incident. There are many internal factors driving change across an organisation. Many individuals speak of culture being (part of) an organisation's DNA[83] and hence slow to change; however, there may be components of that culture that are valid and have a decisive role to play in the organisation's future.

Typically, most cultures change over time to a greater or lesser extent, as the environments in which those organisations work change and the people inside the organisation change as well. We're not going to look at these gradual changes – which may be almost imperceptible – but we should acknowledge and remember that any culture is dynamic.

Instead, we're going to look at planned or reactive cultural change; that moment when someone (or a group of individuals) inside the organisation recognises that part or all of the culture is a problem. A classic example of this is the IBM culture change overseen by Louis Gerstner,[84] where an outsider, brought in at senior level, understood that culture was the problem and needed to change with the help of IBM's employees themselves.

From a security perspective, an incident can be a real signal to senior management that things aren't working; and a learning experience that technology is not the silver bullet they have been sold or led to believe. If the impact has been significant (in terms of business operations, media coverage, or customer feedback) then a well-led organisation will want to understand why and the causes behind the incident. It is at this point that behaviours and values – and questions such as: What did people do? Why did they do something? Why didn't they tell us? Why didn't they do certain things? – can be examined and cultural lessons learned. These can form the basis for the cultural change programme.

I'm regularly engaged by organisations 'post-incident' to help them rethink the human factor. If the board or senior management can resist the impulse to fire someone (typically the CISO) because the breach has happened, then the period after the incident can be very valuable in changing culture.

Organisational culture as a barrier or enabler

The role of culture in delivering more efficient organisational management is a relatively recent consideration from the 1970s.[85] it is recognised that strong cultures can be a barrier to change[86] and significant effort may be needed to make any change stick, including visible changes in leadership, reorganisation of business functions and long-term programmes. A weak culture can be changed but the reverse issue then appears, which is how to embed the changes and then make them stick.[87]

Organisational culture, as something made by human beings, will always have its 'good' and 'bad' characteristics. Note I use quotation marks, as 'good' and 'bad' are determined by personal perspective and the values the observer brings along with them (some may call these 'biases'). Turning these characteristics into levers for change can determine the success or failure of a culture change programme; spotting which of these characteristics can be used to accelerate or reinforce change can also determine whether the culture will be a barrier or enabler.

Within the context of cybersecurity, the question of culture and its role in driving down risk has been talked about for some time, but its relevance has changed. Statutory, regulatory and contractual obligations increasingly specify the need to achieve a security culture. Regulators have clarified that they want to see evidence of the existence of a security culture and the courts routinely point to a lack of, or weak, organisational culture towards cybersecurity, when reviewing data breaches.

CHANGING CULTURE

No matter why we wish to change the culture, it must be run as a programme or project, with people, time and money assigned and objectives set. Importantly, one of the organisation's senior managers, if not the CEO, should be the champion and sponsor of the culture change.

But we must explicitly recognise that culture change will happen at many levels of the organisation – from the board to the newest entry-level employee. So our overall strategy must address change at all the levels – not necessarily at the same time though – to make the changes we are seeking. For our change strategy to have impact, it's often best to start at the top, with the board.

A word of warning – culture change is not taking a group of people away to a nice hotel for a couple of days and coming back with new slogans, titles and buzzwords. These sessions do have their place, especially if a set of values or norms can be created as the basis for a cultural change programme.

We'll deliberately focus on culture change linked to cybersecurity and we'll examine the key components.

Collaborate

I can't stress this enough. Any culture change programme will be the result of a collaborative effort between many individuals, bringing their knowledge, expertise and enthusiasm to the work. You won't be able to do this on your own and such an approach may well doom your efforts to failure. Know your weaknesses and bring in people who can provide the knowledge and expertise to complement your strengths and actively address your weaknesses. As you build your collaborative team to deliver change, make sure you and your team are demonstrating the examples and behaviours you want to be adopted and demonstrated in the organisation.

Create a vision

We hear much talk about vision and strategy for organisations and what those words mean. In our cultural terms, our vision is what we want people to do: the behaviours we would like them to display and the values we would like them to adopt. One stream of thought is to set out challenging and unique values;[88] another is to find those cultural characteristics that are already there and build upon them by reinforcement.

The vision will form part of your toolset to help change the culture. It will be used as the basis of your formal communications and it will set the direction of your change. So, the advice is to keep it simple and memorable.[89]

Involve the board

So how does the board demonstrate the importance of security to its employees, supply chain, customers and other stakeholders?

You can start by looking at what the board and the structure that supports it pay attention to. What is it that they control and measure? And how often do they do this?

By 'paying attention to' I mean a number of things. What forces are driving the board to focus? What topics are discussed and what is the priority given to each? What decisions are they making as to where to bring about change? And then there's the matter of what resources to invest in bringing about that change, and then maintaining and reviewing the security posture within the organisation.

It may seem obvious, but if the board never discuss security, never ask for information about security and only ever talk to the CISO when there is an incident, then other managers will take their cue from the board and ignore security. After all, if the board aren't interested, then why should other managers be interested? Worse still, if the CISO is seen as the 'person you fire after a cyber incident', then other managers will keep their distance, as they don't want to be linked to the CISO by association. You can see the insidious effects of an organisational culture running through this paragraph.

The reverse is also true; if the board take an active interest in any topic, discuss it regularly, then quiz managers about it and require regular reporting, people across the organisation will quickly grasp that the topic is important and actively change to meet the board's requirements and match the board's behaviours.[90]

By 'control', I mean what is it that they have clearly defined as being their expectations when it comes to security? How have they set out their vision, assessed their current position against this and then formulated, implemented and maintained a plan to bridge any gaps? What assessment of the current state of affairs is taking place and what reporting is in place to the board so that they are fully aware of whether their expectations are or are not being met? This is control. Making statements about cybersecurity, including value statements about the importance of cybersecurity, without backing, is little more than window dressing.

Obtain investment

Investment in security is a possible means of evidencing the embedding of cybersecurity into an organisation's culture or, as a minimum, it is evidence of how the board can clearly demonstrate how seriously it takes the matter.

When thinking about investment within the context of cybersecurity, don't limit your vision or interpretation of this to how much in terms of £s, €s or $s is being spent or you would like to be spent, the technology you can acquire or the increase in your security budget. We are talking about different aspects of investment:[91] the slow and careful commitment of resources using well-understood tools and techniques to achieve a defined aim; the personal act of spending your time and your efforts to achieve change.

It's worth examining what is driving the decision to consider investment and, importantly, the process for making that decision, as well as the actual capital or operational spend. In terms of decision drivers, the key will be to understand the drivers for the board and senior management, both as a group and individually. These drivers will be many, varied and even contradictory; they may have external and internal influences; and they may be personal. Each board member or senior manager will have their own decision process, their own biases and heuristics and their own judgement on the value of making the investment. All of these will come together to create a decision backed by the board.[92]

> Try to keep an open mind and remember that it is quite likely that different boards, especially in different cultures, will interpret the word 'investment' slightly differently, but probably with some common denominators.

In terms of drivers for investment, what is driving the board to look at the issue of security culture? Is it an actual security incident their organisation has experienced? Is it to address a strategic barrier to entering or operating in a particular market? Is it in response to a level of self-awareness about corporate responsibility to customers and more broadly society? Or is this about corporate resilience in a digitally reliant world? Or has the regulator told them?

Each one of these questions and answers says something about the priorities and arguably the values the board associates with security. Mishandled, they can act as a lightning strike that drives a wedge between what is said and what is actually done. This is the cultural dissonance I spoke about in the previous chapter. Handled well they can act as a rallying point giving certainty and assurance about what is socially acceptable within the organisation and the group of colleagues you interact with to 'get things done'.

What does it say about leadership, where the board make a decision to invest having thoroughly assessed the business case, based on an understanding of the risk to the organisation's key strategic key performance indicators (KPIs), compared to a board who conduct a benchmarking exercise against other organisations with a similar profile in the same industry? It is not unusual for organisational boards to ask advisory and consultancy practices to share insights into what other similar organisations are doing and investing.

Another comparison would be investment based on the need to comply with regulatory and statutory obligations where the minimum is done to get the organisation compliant and possibly certified. But when you set out with the objective of doing the minimum possible to get your organisation over the line of compliance, what does that say to those most closely involved in the programme, and those who you seek to influence across the organisation? Does it sound like security is really important and that it is truly valued by the board and the wider organisation? Probably, no.

Respond in times of crisis

Another telling sign of whether the security values are embedded within the organisation's culture is how the board and senior management respond in a crisis or incident. As many security professionals can relate, many people in organisations from the top to the bottom just do not believe a 'cyberattack will happen to us', with many reasons given from 'we're too small' to 'we have nothing of value' to 'we're better than the organisation that got hit'.

Much of this thinking can be attributed to biases and heuristics and their role in forming and influencing behaviours. We have a number of biases[93] that apply when we think. In terms of cybersecurity, two biases can affect our thinking and our approach to incidents. The first is the salience (or saliency) bias, which describes our tendency to focus on items or information that are more noteworthy while ignoring those that do not grab our attention.[94] A great example is that as cybersecurity professionals we focus on incidents as they are of personal interest to us, whereas clothing fashion professionals will probably focus on what they are wearing rather than incidents for the same reason. Another bias is the normalcy bias,[95] which is the refusal to plan for or react to a disaster that has never happened before; in our case a cyber incident. And finally, there is the availability heuristic (see Tversky and Kahneman, 1973), in which we recall something similar to the event we are either discussing or being told about. Unfortunately, for many non-security people, the likelihood of a security incident seems distant. Presenting data that illustrates the frequency with which these incidents occur is a step forward to influencing people; but we also fight against these biases until something happens to them (or their peer group).

If the leadership team appear to not be in control in the wake of an incident, then many will question the seriousness placed on the matter of security in the first place. This is because several assumptions will be made.

- The organisation wasn't aware – in which case why not? After all, ignorance is no defence.
- The organisation was aware but was in denial – this may be considered negligence.
- The organisation was aware and had a plan but it failed – this may be considered bad luck.
- The organisation was aware and had a plan that worked – great leadership and foresight (or just plain lucky).

When an organisation has a crisis, even if they have incident management plans, crisis management plans and so on, they will have to face two interrelated issues. First, the plan probably won't cover the actual incident;[96] second, no matter the roles assigned, there will always be someone (probably senior) who wants to take over and 'be in charge', regardless of whether that is the right action in the circumstances. The first can be solved easily through regular exercises using the plan, so that all participants view it as a framework to help them manage the incident. The second is less easy to solve, as senior managers tend not to participate in exercises and (by their very nature) want to be in control and leading the team.

We've also touched on the 'CISO as fall guy' approach, which basically results in the CISO being fired if an incident happens, regardless of whether the CISO or the organisation were capable of detecting and responding to the incident. This is a powerful indication of the culture and of the values of the organisation.

We can examine two changes to our culture. The first is to overcome the biases we have been talking about and to acknowledge that an incident could happen and to have a plan to handle it when it does.

The second is to build a culture where reporting suspected incidents (including data breaches) is seen as the 'right thing'. We mentioned the significant number of data breaches being reported in the European Union since the introduction of GDPR in an earlier chapter. But is this increase because (suddenly) individuals and organisations have become worse at handling personal data? Has there been a sudden spike in incidents? Or has there always been this level of incidents but organisations and their employees didn't feel either a moral or a legal obligation to report these before? Did they even reach out to the data subjects affected or make an effort to understand the likely risk to them of a failure in their own systems of control? The values that drive decisions like these, whether to report and communicate incidents, for example, are the values that lay the foundation for the role of cybersecurity within an organisation's culture. We can and should seek to build a culture where reporting is valued and individuals are rewarded for noticing odd or strange activities and behaviours.

Culturally, responding to crises becomes not about pointing the finger of blame; it's about acknowledging shortcomings in the processes in place and guaranteeing you'll address those.

Challenge assumptions

In my early days within the security industry, before the phrase 'cybersecurity' was used, I routinely asked clients to look at their contracts with both suppliers and customers. Almost always the contract would have a condition requiring a third party to make assurances about confidentiality or a condition where the client made a statement assuring a customer about confidentiality. I'd then ask them on what grounds they could make such a promise or put their name on a contract that made it contractually binding. Back then the response was consistently the same, irrespective of who I was talking to. Whether at a board or, back then, the IT level, commonly there was no answer or an assumption that it was sorted, although by whom and how was not known. At worst, they didn't really care. At best I was given a list of tactical interventions, from IT controls to HR and legal.

Where an organisation's leadership's sense of control is based on broad assumptions, this illustrates potential vulnerabilities in their overall control of the issues at hand. Where a board see the issue as someone else's responsibility, like the security, IT, risk and compliance functions, this reinforces a sense that incidents that arise aren't the organisation's responsibility, but down to IT, cybersecurity, risk and compliance. Traditionally these functions only make up a small part of the overall workforce.

This approach 'that someone else is taking care of it' raises some interesting cultural insights. Among the insights are that: the organisation is very rigid – people do exactly what they are told and exactly what their job description says; 'stepping out of line' or 'asking questions' may be disliked or actively discouraged; and silo behaviour and silo thinking predominate. For topics such as information security that require cross-functional thinking and behaviours, this culture can be a real challenge to building all three of the ABCs.

Allocate resources

Is there a dedicated resource focused on improving or supporting the improvement of the organisation's overall security posture?

> I often find myself challenging clients about what they actually mean when they use the term 'dedicated'. It may seem self-explanatory but, in my experience, people use or interpret common terms like this inconsistently. I've experienced 'dedicated' resources who have been dedicated to the responsibility but carry this alongside several other responsibilities. I've experienced 'dedicated' resources who have been given the responsibility but are not measured against the delivery of this or who have not been given the resources or support to implement what they want to get done.

To be clear, culture change takes time and requires resource and expertise. When we talk about dedicated resource, we are talking about ring-fenced budget items and, more importantly, people who can spend the majority of their time (say 75 per cent plus) on the culture change programme. Not only that, the programme has milestones and measures to assess progress and success.

Does security have a budget or is it a matter of resources being made available on an as and when basis? The existence of a budget may be interpreted as illustrating the importance of security to the organisation. After all, the investment is a decision to invest in the future; it is a commitment, instead of investment based on responding to business needs that arrive on an ad hoc basis, which has a feel of 'let's see if we can get away with it' about it. But money is only part of the story.[97] Unfortunately, by creating a line item, or setting out a budget for security, it is then easy for people to say, 'Look! We invest in security!' However, as is well known, much of the security budget goes on tools and the people running them[98] and there isn't much room for the non-technical side of information security. In part, this spending on tools is to show a tangible return (you gave us 'X', we bought 'Y') but, I think, reflects the typical technology-led approach we see in cybersecurity. It is easier to buy a tool than to explain, justify and then purchase a 'soft' culture change programme.

Another common assumption, and therefore mistake regarding resource allocation, is that other stakeholders across the organisation will respond positively and facilitate everything the security function needs to bring about a change in organisational culture. Going back to the discussion earlier about what people perceive to be important and how that is driven from the top, and our discussions about the fact that cybersecurity just doesn't register for many people, you have to tackle the 'Why should I bother?' If you can't make the case that helping you will help those stakeholders, your work will be met with polite indifference or outright hostility.

Role modelling by the board

How does the board and senior management team provide deliberate role modelling themselves and throughout the organisational structure? In other words, do the board and the senior management team 'live' security, or ideally values closely associated with security attributes, in a very visible way through everything they do?

Getting visibly involved in cybersecurity initiatives as a figurehead seems to be the level of ambition of many. It's something I always like to see done. Unfortunately, not all organisations have one or more senior individuals willing to become the figurehead for cybersecurity. Without such a visible individual, it becomes harder to make the case for cybersecurity, as we have discussed earlier.

A figurehead on their own doesn't make much difference. You should plan on how to use your figurehead across the ABCs and as a key role model in your culture change programme. In some ways, I would suggest that you sort out your programme and then appoint a figurehead; hopefully they will be enthused by the programme and act as both a supporter and an advocate as part of their role. It may be better for your potential figurehead to understand what they are signing up to in terms of your programme **before** they front it, rather than signing the individual up first and then developing your programme. Be careful, as well, of having a figurehead and then not supporting them. If people are willing to help, remember to reciprocate and provide them with information, take time to talk to them and equip them with the information they feel they need to be credible and useful. If you don't, you will lose your figurehead and you will also see a degree of cynicism and a lack of appetite to help you in the future. This is a two-way relationship.

Role modelling is both a conscious and unconscious activity. People in all walks of life at all stages act as role models, sometimes unknowingly. And unconsciously or consciously, people are drawn to and influenced by these.

As a young teenager who loved sports, and played for the school, I distinctly remember admiring those who played in the more senior rugby and athletics teams. I remember the inspiration I got when a sixth former handed me a pair of running spikes for my 100 metres race and explained why they'd be of help. Or the full back for the school's first XV rugby team who sat down and talked me through how he played the role and invited me to watch when the team played a home game.

As I mentioned in the previous chapter, our choices, and the behavioural outcomes from these, are heavily influenced by what we see others doing around us. We are naturally, and subconsciously, tuned to mimic the behaviours we encounter day to day, especially those that belong to a person we might aspire to be, or that appear to result in recognition, success or both.

Setting an example through role modelling is one way of leveraging this subconscious-primed response within the human. Leaders may acknowledge that this is the case, but do they consciously fulfil their 'role model' roles? Or is their approach 'do as I say, not as I do'? For example, do they follow the organisational policies, processes and procedures where it suits them but bend these when the situation doesn't suit their needs and purposes, and do others around them experience this? If they don't follow the rules, can they be held to account and will they be?

We should also acknowledge the fact that not all role models are exemplars of following the rules, good behaviour and cultural norms.[99] In fact, these individuals are sometimes required to break previous cultural norms to help reset or change the organisational culture.

Build rewards and recognition

How does the leadership team and operational management recognise appropriate behaviours and reward these? This includes enhancing the status of individuals who have demonstrated behaviours that are in line with cultural values.

The MAS report quoted above also suggests that 'Staff [are] recognised for exemplifying financial institution's values',[100] and this taps into a wider discussion about how we can reward individuals who display the ABCs in a positive matter. Over the years we've all heard and participated in discussions about tying people's pay rises and bonuses (or components thereof) to cybersecurity achievements or milestones. An example of this approach can be seen in the context of health and safety where a bonus is awarded if a stated number of accident-free days is exceeded on a site, coupled with evidence of regular training and awareness. Interestingly, I've never heard a discussion where the same model should be applied to cybersecurity professionals.[101]

Of course, the issue here is multifaceted. Let's just focus on five components: measurement, legal, human resources (HR) and culture:

- Do we have the capability to measure everyone's behaviour and specifically security-related behaviour all of the time they are at work, irrespective of location?

- Legally, can we monitor, track, record and then openly publish people's behaviour?[102]

- Can we have the same set of rules, rewards and punishments globally?

- How comfortable are we as cybersecurity professionals and the organisation in pinpointing and calling out individuals for security errors or breaches and then tying that to promotions, monetary rewards and bad publicity for breaching the security norms?

- Does the organisation really care about cybersecurity that much to do all this and change the reward structure?

It's the answer to the last question that often means this idea is a non-starter. Simply, the answer is no.

So instead if thinking in terms of punishment, let's turn to reward. We've mentioned that positive reinforcement is a much more powerful tool, and there are many examples of cybersecurity staff leaving balloons, chocolates and other rewards on people's desks where they have demonstrated a security behaviour (such as locking a laptop or having a clean desk). As part of our cultural change, these are important symbols, rewards that can serve as the basis for stories and myths. However, we need more than just chocolates. When we think about rewards and recognition, we are likely to focus on the behavioural aspects and outcomes, as these are readily visible and easy to communicate. But don't forget that culture is more than just behaviours.

If we wish to develop or change rewards and recognition, then we'll need to work with the board, human resources (or equivalent) and the internal communications functions. Obviously, when we think about rewards, especially those that involve money or personnel records, we need to engage stakeholders to understand how reward systems work and how we can work with HR to record good behaviours, reward them through the appraisal and review systems, or reward them through other approaches (such as spot cash rewards) and so on. If employee recognition systems are used, then we need to understand how recognition is performed, the systems used to capture recommendations and then communicate the recognition to the employee and the wider organisation. We also need to work with the internal communications team to understand the style and frequency of reward and recognition communications.

Finally, we need to decide what we are going to reward. Behaviours are a good choice, as we can describe a situation, describe what happened and then discuss the behaviours shown and why those behaviours are worthy of reward. It is more difficult to reward the intangible aspects of culture as it can be more difficult to identify and describe them and draw out clear messages.

Recruit and retain

How does the recruitment process reflect the importance of the cultural values associated with security? What role does an individual's values, skills and attributes associated with security play in their selection for promotion or for getting their first job at the organisation?

It is a truism that many organisations – for example, financial institutions, technology companies and consultancies – recruit a 'certain type of person'. The people they recruit often possess and demonstrate some or many of the behaviours and values the organisations want and which are already part of the culture. You can also correctly argue that individuals with certain cultural backgrounds and values will want to apply to these same institutions. This recruitment bias can lead to 'monocultures'[103] where cultural fit and shared values become ingrained and unchallenged.

It is a further truism that beyond cybersecurity job adverts, very few adverts call for cybersecurity values, skills, experience or cultural aspects. Interviews are typically used to explore cultural fit between the candidate and the organisation but – again – if security isn't part of the culture, then it won't be explored in the interview.

An aside and one that I feel is representative of our cybersecurity culture is the language and values we often use and describe in job adverts for cybersecurity roles. The words tend to be technical, masculine and individualistic; there can be the use of words linked to conflict and war. We should also look at ourselves and ask if we are expressing the right culture and values in our words and adverts; and if we really are attracting the candidates we say we want to attract. The words we use in our adverts may be unattractive to 50 per cent of the candidate pool. If that 50 per cent doesn't apply, then we have already cut ourselves off from a lot of good people.

Stories, myths and legends

In the previous chapter I explained the role of both formal and informal education processes and institutions. In addition to these education processes, we also learn through storytelling. Every culture contains stories, myths and legends, and the power of storytelling is something that many within the security industry will have heard as a means to effectively raise awareness and influence behaviour towards an appropriate culture.

Humans seem to be hardwired in the brain to respond positively to storytelling. Well, good storytelling at least. Good storytelling bridges the gap between a simple narrative and an emotional connection that makes it all come to life. Context, or the plot of a story, turbo-charges words to draw us in, engage us successfully and improve the odds of something being remembered, retold and acted upon.[104]

Some myths and legends are introduced and fostered deliberately, and some seem to grow on their own, among personnel over time. Some are true, others are half-truths and some are fabrications. What some people remember, and subconsciously use to define what is or is not acceptable, may not even have happened to them. It might be something they heard that has become anchored in their subconscious as a truth by the organisation or state, as part of fostering the values and ideals that it aspires to or believes it embodies. It's not dissimilar to developing a brand and then the process of making this come alive within an organisation. These values tend to be passed from person to person, even through generations, and to be done in an almost organic, informal way.

Formal statements

In the previous chapter I mentioned artefacts and espoused values. These are formal statements of the organisation's philosophy when it comes to cybersecurity. They cover values or attributes such as confidentiality, integrity and availability, associated with information, systems and processes; they may also state the behaviours we wish people to adopt and demonstrate.

These come in the shape of policies, processes and procedures. You'll find them communicated through formal internal communication campaigns or permanently added to the environment within which we work. It's worth stepping back and considering the general level of knowledge about policies, processes and procedures, and then to consider the level of knowledge about the IT and cybersecurity policies, processes and procedures. In my experience, the two most read policies in most organisations are the holiday policy ('How much time can I get off work?') and the expense policy ('What can I claim and how much can I get back?'); most people in an organisation wouldn't even know there are IT and cybersecurity policies published and would have no idea where to find them or who to ask, even if they wanted to read them. And, let's be honest, most IT and cybersecurity policies are not great reads.[105]

So, the reach of our formal statements as expressed in organisational policies is limited. There are other formal communications we can use, such as corporate newsletters, training, emails and so on but all of these have their limitations.

The best mechanism for driving cultural change is to take these formal statements and live and demonstrate them. This neatly ties back into our discussion of role modelling: making the culture a tangible thing so that people can see it, understand it and shape their behaviours to match.

We can also take key messages and turn them into slogans as part of a communication campaign. This is of course where we need to work with communications specialists, alongside our other specialists, to develop the simple and effective messaging that accompanies the changes we wish to make.

Job titles and responsibilities

It is widely accepted that there is a general skills and experience shortage in the security industry. However, this is amplified when it comes to finding candidates for job roles where raising awareness, influencing behaviour and fostering an appropriate organisational culture are the key objectives.

The shortage is highlighted as a result of an increase in demand from CISOs and the organisations they represent. This demand is driven by a number of factors. First, there has been an increase in statutory, regulatory and even contractual obligations regarding security education and awareness. The European Union's GDPR as well as industry standards, such as ISO/IEC 27001,[106] NIST Framework for Improving Critical Infrastructure Cybersecurity[107] and PCI DSS v3.2.1,[108] all place a requirement for organisations to implement demonstrable education and awareness activities.

Second, as we have mentioned previously, many contracts between organisations now include clauses demanding that suppliers can demonstrate the existence of an education and awareness programme designed to reduce risky data security and privacy behaviour. Having a job role bearing the title education and awareness or security culture manager is one way to tick the box.

Third, regulators', the law court's and even media's interpretation of the role of culture and its link with security and privacy breaches is routinely made clear. Cultural attitudes, starting from the board down, are often highlighted as the root cause of many of the breaches investigated. The lack of an appropriate culture is often part of the reasoning behind penalties administered by the courts and regulators. It's also a key element within media reporting post-incident.

With this in mind, organisations need to be seen to take this seriously. Rightly or wrongly, taking this seriously starts, for many, by creating a specific role with responsibility for this. Then there's the matter of finding an appropriate person to fill the role. This is driving the increase in job vacancies and roles where security awareness, behaviour and culture are part of the job title or specification.

To be effective, as we have discussed earlier, the role must be assigned resources and the time for the programme to deliver. Merely giving someone the title will not improve any of the ABCs.

SUMMARY

Creating or changing a culture is a human-oriented endeavour. Just as culture is formed by people interacting, it is changed by the same thing. We've explored a lot in this chapter, from models of organisational change to collaboration and job titles in the context of changing culture.

Changing culture requires effort, the use of many tools, differing knowledge sets and the ability to understand both the tangible and the intangible; behaviours, values and their interactions; and the understanding of how to use a range of tools to express what has to change and to provide the impetus to change.

There is no one best way to change your organisational culture, nor is there one good reason why you should do so. If you embark on the culture change journey, there are many factors to consider and we would urge you to use this chapter as your guidebook to help you map out that journey and to help orient you as you travel onwards.

NEXT STEPS

It's often said that practice makes perfect, so we suggest some actions you can take below:

1. Identify a behaviour or value you would like to change.

2. Describe what your ideal changed behaviour or value would look like.

3. Draw up a roadmap of how you would like to change the behaviour or value.

4. Identify who can help and when you need help.

5. Define your measurements to show the change has stuck.

8 WHERE NEXT?

Adrian Davis

Our theme throughout this book has been that cybersecurity is about people – and that people can be the best asset to protect a business and its information. But information security awareness, behaviour and culture are but one of many competing priorities for both the CISO and the business. Given this fact, and all the constraints we are under, how can we develop, enhance and elevate our ability to deliver the ABCs?

Many guides to awareness programmes have been produced, exhorting the CISO to do this or do that, measure this or measure that. It would be easy to follow precedent and set out such a guide in this chapter. Our approach is somewhat different. Our belief is that the three components – awareness, behaviour and culture – work hand in hand to change people's attitude, activities and involvement with cyber or information security. So rather than exhorting you to produce new slides, write clearer messages and target your work (which are all certainly relevant and need to be done), we're going to take a different approach: start with and apply the ABCs to yourselves.

At this point, I hope you are asking why. Why do we personally need security awareness? We are the teachers, the professionals and the experts. Well, before we try to change anything or anybody, we need to look at ourselves. We cannot force people to change or be convincing proponents of change if we haven't changed ourselves and, most importantly, made those changes 'stick'. In other words, we have changed our behaviour and have accepted those changes; integrated them into our thinking and our day-to-day activities; and those changes have become long term and second nature. They have become unconscious: we don't think about the changes, we just do them. Building on our discussion of culture in the previous chapters, I'll hope you'll recognise that we have changed our culture as well.

START WITH YOU

To apply the ABCs, we start with ourselves. It is little use to change something if we don't know where we are starting from, as we won't know what's changed. We also start by asking a simple question: what is our culture (or rather the culture of the security function in the business)? How do we behave? What do we say and how do we say it? Much of business is personal, an oft-forgotten fact, and people react and behave according to the people around them. If we as security professionals do not live or demonstrate the awareness, behaviours and culture we want other people to copy and adopt, then we can hardly blame them if they don't show those very same behaviours themselves. If we cannot understand other cultures and norms in the organisation and try to impose our own culture and norms on top, or in place of those other organisational cultures and norms, then we will fail. In fact, in a large organisation, the sheer number of non-security professionals may be seen to doom us to failure. As an example, one organisation your author has worked at has over 500,000 (yes, over half a million) people working for it globally: the total number of IT and security staff globally was about 1,000; we can hardly dominate, and pushing our culture is a challenge. We will come back to the numbers game later.

When we talk about living behaviours, I'm not saying we should all be rushing around in 'superhero' costumes and acting as if we are the guardians of the corporate galaxy. Nor am I saying we need to be like everybody else. To make the ABCs work we need to embody what we say, teach and do. We need to constantly check ourselves and our behaviours and ensure how and what we do sends and reinforces the messages we want. We may have to alter our mindsets and our approach to problems so that we fit in better with the corporate culture and way of doing things. This is very hard, as it requires reflection, feedback and time – and time is often at a premium. It's also very difficult to change and admit our weaknesses; yet that is a vital part of any change programme. I'm not going to peddle 'cod psychology' here with some four-step process to reach enlightenment. Instead, apply the tools and insights in this book – and find out how change works from the experts.

On top of our relentless focus on ourselves, we need to make a long-term commitment to understand the organisational culture, our place in it and to then create our own culture that fits into the organisation yet delivers the cybersecurity the business needs. This is perhaps the most important decision we have to make. It's easy as a cybersecurity professional to look at an organisation and dismiss the level of security as 'rubbish' or 'just not good enough'. However, the level of cyber (and indeed physical) security an organisation has, needs, should have and what we think it should have may be very different. Factors such as the industry sector (our experience in one sector may not transfer well to another sector), the business understanding and commitment to cybersecurity and the decisions made by the business will all influence the security that is in place and the attitude to cybersecurity. Ultimately, the business that pays for the cybersecurity may have deliberately decided to have a particular level of security. No matter what we think, the business will usually have the final say. A good example is a finance or profit focused organisation where hitting financial targets are the pre-eminent decision-making criteria: anything that pushes up costs, reduces margin, reduces profit and is not seen as core to the business will not receive much support. In terms of the ABCs, we need to cut our cloth accordingly; there is no point in trying to build elaborate schemes if the business doesn't want them, nor will it support them. This of course comes back to culture and our understanding of the organisation, and how we fit our culture and our norms within the organisation.

So, the ABCs don't start with glossy new presentations and merch, followed by swift behavioural interventions and the creation of a security culture. They start with us, our behaviour and culture, and an awareness of our place in the organisation and how we fit into the corporate culture. Once we understand that fit between security and the business, and hopefully have made strides ourselves to close any gaps, then we can start the real journey. However much we don't like it, we have to change to fit ourselves into the existing culture and the business, not the other way round.

The real journey is change. The ultimate results of the ABCs are change: change in and of ourselves and change in non-security people's perceptions, thoughts and actions so that they perform work (and non-work) activities in what we, as security professionals, consider to be a more secure manner. Change, as discussed, is incredibly hard to make happen and to then take forward.

So, going back to the previous paragraphs, we have to change first. Once we understand culture and have improved our awareness and insights into culture, then we can plan change. It's tempting to go for big changes and radical solutions; but these may not be the ones that work or stick. Sometimes, it's better to go small. Small changes are often easier to make and easier to keep going.

FOCUS ON WHY

Instead of rushing in and trying to change anything and everything, we should focus on the simple question posed by Jessica in Chapter 2: why?

If we can answer that question in a convincing and simple manner, then we can start our journey. We shouldn't try to answer that question on our own; that would be one of the biggest mistakes we could make. Instead, we should ask that question to a representative cross-section of our organisation from top to bottom and use that to help us answer the why. It will also help us to understand what people know, want to learn and want help with; all of which are inputs into the design of a successful change programme. We are raising our awareness – we are focusing our attention on culture and our fit within the organisation and its culture. We're not trying to change anything yet: remembering the definition of awareness, we're becoming aware.

> Interestingly, awareness is also the first step in some marketing campaigns and forms part of AIDA: awareness, interest, desire and action. The underlying concept in AIDA is that by creating awareness, we can then build interest, create desire and drive action. In fact, AIDA is another tool that is applicable here and across all the ABCs.[109]

Asking 'why' on its own will, in all likelihood, provide us with a dazzling array of answers and many of those may not be actually relevant to the question. We actually need to structure the question slightly more subtly to capture the information we need. We could ask questions such as 'why don't you engage with our security awareness programmes?', 'why do you have a negative perception of the security function?', 'why do you think the information security function is viewed negatively in your department' – and so on. Asking the reverse – 'what do you find interesting in our awareness campaigns?', 'what do you like about working with us?' – help us capture and understand the approaches we should be doing more of. These questions, with their open nature and their appeal to the less rational and more emotional side of the individual, should help to capture the insights we need to examine what and how we do things. Don't be afraid to follow up these questions with further questions such as 'what makes our programmes dull and uninteresting?', 'what would you change?' to gain further insight. Again, we can focus on the positive – 'would you like more of this style of training?', 'do you want us to attend more project meetings?' – to balance the insights we gather and help us to build a fuller picture of how and where we are succeeding and how and where we are not. You'll be surprised at how much people will share because they have been asked, especially if the interview is face to face and the individual is in a junior role.

This may be an extremely uncomfortable exercise – after all, these questions may reveal some pretty harsh perceptions about us and what we do – but it is necessary to fully understand where we are starting from and where we can change. The answers need to be analysed and it may be valuable to bring in one or two individuals from outside the function to help with that analysis and provide a different (though it may not be objective) perspective.

IDENTIFY BEHAVIOURS

Equipped with these insights and some deep thinking about what they mean, we can continue our ABC journey. Now we are aware, we have to translate that into action. We've already intimated that it's best to start small when considering changes: small changes typically are easier to make and thus often will be made; small changes tend to be more 'sticky', which means that once the change is made, people don't go back and undo the change they've just made. Think about quitting an addiction or starting exercise. Both require major changes in lifestyle, behaviours and may challenge established social groups and norms, which is why people often find it difficult to make these changes and then keep going. Now think about recycling paper at work. Typically, there are paper recycling points in many offices, so people recycle paper because it is easy to do so and actually is not a major change – instead of throwing it in the bin, you walk the short distance to the recycling point. It's a small change requiring little thought or effort to perform and then repeat. So again, rather than tell you to radically change your entire function, awareness programmes and the way you do things, we'll adopt a different tack.

The key approach here is to identify the good behaviours and keep reinforcing them. Everyone reacts better to praise than criticism, so turn that to your advantage. Additionally, the more you reward good behaviours, the elusive positive feedback loop will start to appear: good behaviours are rewarded, which encourages further good behaviours, which are rewarded and so on.

Unwanted or negative behaviours will have to be addressed; they can't be ignored. As good behaviours become increasingly the norm, it will be easier to spot the unwanted or negative behaviours and deal with them. There will be a tipping point where such unwanted or negative behaviours are spotted by everyone involved and actions taken to correct them.

It can be beneficial to step back and think through the behaviours that we want to encourage or praise and these can be linked back to our 'why'. We should try to link the behaviours to meeting the why; and try to model what those behaviours look like in practice.

An important concept to use here is the 'moment of truth'. Jan Carlzon, the CEO of SAS,[110] wrote a book quite a few years ago (Carlzon, 1987), in which he described how every time a customer interacts with a service, that interaction allows the customer to form an impression. That impression can be positive or negative – and people tend to share negative impressions. Carlzon proposed that every interaction should be managed to create a positive outcome. This was applied across SAS, which rose to become one of the most admired airlines by its peers at one point. The idea has been picked up and expanded by Proctor & Gamble and even Google to bring it into the consumer goods and internet shopping spaces. In terms of our thinking and behaviours, we can look at the interactions we have with the rest of the organisation and decide how to change the interaction and the associated behaviours to make the outcome positive. It's more than stopping saying 'no' (which is way too simplistic, although it helps); it's thinking how we change what and how we do things, so that every interaction is positive. That doesn't mean we solve everything there and then, but if we can't solve an issue, we take positive steps to do so – even if it is 'I'll call you tomorrow and let you know what I've found out' and we do so. This approach shouldn't be confused with feedback surveys and 'rate your experience' approaches, rather it is something more fundamental and behaviour driven.

Once behaviours start to change, culture will start to change as well. Culture, as we have seen, is made up of many things: artefacts, attitudes, practices and shared values. As our practices (behaviours) change, our culture will start to change. It may be imperceptible at first, but once one part of the mix changes, then other changes start to happen.

These changes can be supported by careful intervention to reinforce and change other parts of the culture mix. It's often said that you set the 'tone at the top' and leadership and the way in which senior people behave do set out particular boundaries and styles of behaviour that influence and are copied by other staff.

Key among the relevant artefacts will be the stories – the tales that encapsulate good behaviours and actions that should be emulated. All cybersecurity professionals have a fund of war stories and it isn't too difficult to pick and share stories that highlight the wanted behaviours.

The CISO thus has a many-hatted role in the security function's ABC journey. The CISO may be leading the whole initiative, so has to be the leader and cheerleader for the initiative. The CISO may be the embodiment of the changes required, so has to be the role model all of the time (which is a lot tougher than you think); the CISO may also be the coach, helping people through change by rewarding wanted behaviours and spotting unwanted behaviours; and, if the ABC journey is being led by another staff member, the CISO may be part of the team.

It has often been said that cybersecurity is 'a marathon, not a sprint'. The ABCs are a marathon and it is fair to say that there is no defined end; organisations change, as do their culture(s), so the security function has to be able to change with the organisation. The security function should regularly check using the ABCs that they are still aligned to the organisation. When we come to apply the ABCs to the wider organisation, we are most definitely going to be involved in a classical marathon.[111]

Of course, there is another reason for going through the ABCs ourselves. It is so much easier to lead change, explain change and make change happen if you have been through the process and have experienced the effects of change yourself. We can apply what we have learned to our security awareness programmes to make them more effective and to start the ABC journey for the organisation.

Applying the ABCs

At the start of this book, we displayed the 'ABC wheel' and we pointed out that the three components (awareness, behaviour and culture) are intimately linked (Figure 8.1).

Figure 8.1 Simple cybersecurity ABC model

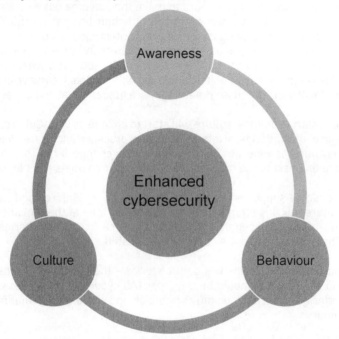

When it comes to applying the ABCs to the organisation, the guiding principle as mentioned earlier should be to start small. I have said that you won't be exhorted to produce new slides, write clearer messages and target your work. Instead, before you start, write down what you want the awareness message, programme, project, communication or presentation to actually achieve.

Using the 'ABC wheel' in Figure 8.1 reminds us that when we set out to create an awareness message, we should consider its impact on behaviour and culture; likewise, we should consider the impact of current behaviour and current culture on that awareness message. A moment's reflection, for example, on how language is used – a cultural artefact as you may remember – will help you to choose the right words in your message, or the right headline for a particular slide. Further reflection on the behaviour you are trying to change may lead you to a more positive message and, perhaps, an appeal to the more emotional perspectives of your staff.

Let's go through two practical examples where we can use the ABCs and their integration to create awareness messages (Table 8.1).

Table 8.1 Planning templates incorporating the ABCs

Example 1: USB devices

Questions and outcomes	Insights and messages
What we want to happen	People follow our policy and don't plug USB devices into organisational devices
What are the current behaviours?	There is a mix:
	Some people are plugging USB devices into company IT devices
	Some people are sending USB sticks to IT
	Some people are throwing USB sticks away
	Some people are asking if they can plug in USB external drives
What is the current culture?	Trust in people's judgement
	Work collaboratively and help each other to succeed
	Work flexibly; embrace new technologies to deliver better
	It's only IT (a 'shadow culture')
What is the current message?	'Follow the policy, don't plug in USB sticks to your work computer'
Why isn't the current message working?	Too narrow
	Goes against the 'use your judgement' and 'work flexibly'
	A perception that if the IT is broken, then the IT function will fix it, so there are no repercussions
How we are going to deliver	Focus the message. Get the messaging about USB sticks right and understood in the first round of the campaign
	1. Awareness: 'USB sticks may contain all sorts of information and apps. Some of those apps may damage or destroy information on your laptop or desktop'
	2. Behaviour change: 'We know, altruistically, if you find a USB stick, you may want to find who owns it – so you may plug it into your computer to find out the owner *but* no matter where you got a USB stick from, even colleagues, friends and family, *please* don't plug it into your work computer. Send it to IT or call us if you are unsure'
	3. Culture: play on the 'work collaboratively and help each other to succeed'

(Continued)

Table 8.1 (Continued)

Example 1: USB devices

Questions and outcomes	Insights and messages
Our new key messages	1. Awareness: 'Don't be tempted and don't take the chance'
	2. Behaviour: 'Call us and send the USB stick to IT'
	3. Culture: 'Remember your act of kindness may cost someone else their weekend'. That's not how we work collaboratively nor how we succeed, so reinforce the 'help each other to succeed'
How we are going to deliver the key message(s) – face to face, CBT, merchandise, etc.	Posters in public spaces
	Face-to-face presentations to IT during team meetings
	Slide for staff meetings and face-to-face talk where possible
	Check induction programme to emphasise USB policy
Who we need to communicate with – senior or junior roles, IT or non-IT or a mixture	IT – they set the example
	Junior staff – we know they use USBs a lot
	Senior staff – policy; follow the rules
New behaviour	Call IT
	Send the USB stick to IT
Culture change	'Don't plug that in! That's not helping anybody'
	Norm is **not** to plug USB in; staff actively stop each other doing it
What success looks like	Fewer reported issues to helpdesk
	Reduction in malware infections
	More questions and calls to helpdesk and security staff about USB
	USB sticks arriving at IT in the internal post
Other factors for success	Make sure IT are OK with the new message and behaviour
	IT has a sandbox PC to plug USB devices into
	Thank you email
	Helpdesk script
	Random card, chocolate or balloon drop on the desks of people who have sent USB sticks to IT

(Continued)

Table 8.1 (Continued)

Example 2: Remote working

Questions and outcomes	Insights and messages
What we want to happen	A significant majority of remote users using their work laptop
What are the current behaviours?	There is a mix:
	We know that people use a mix of work and non-work computers to login when remotely working
	People download work-related material to non-work computers
What is the current culture?	'I need to grab my email but the work laptop takes ages'
	'Security gets in the way'
	'But it's only email, it's not like it's important'
What is the current message?	'Log in, use a virtual private network never use your home computer'
Why isn't the current message working?	Log in and connection are seen as slow and overly difficult
How we are going to deliver	1. Awareness: 'We build our computers to protect you and the business. Use the tools we give you'
	'We know login is slow and annoying but it's all there for a reason. By going through the process you are making all of us safer'
	2. Behaviour change: 'Always use my work laptop'
	3. Culture: play on the 'doing things right'
Our new key messages	1. Awareness: 'Work stays with work. Don't mix business and pleasure'
	2. Behaviour: 'Always use your work laptop'
	3. Culture: 'Speed is irrelevant. Doing it right is what matters'
How we are going to deliver the key message(s) – face to face, CBT, merchandise, etc.	Posters in public spaces
	Face-to-face presentations to IT during team meetings
	Slide for staff meetings and face-to face-talk where possible
	Check induction programme to emphasise using work equipment

(Continued)

Table 8.1 (Continued)

Example 2: Remote working

Questions and outcomes	Insights and messages
Who we need to communicate with – senior or junior roles, IT or non-IT or a mixture	Everyone
New behaviour	Always use your work laptop
Culture change	If it is work-related, it stays on work computers
What success looks like	Users logging in via their work computers
	More virtual private network (VPN) connections
Other factors for success	Make sure IT and network ops can handle the increased VPN use
	Longer term – single sign on so the VPN automatically starts and connects

Using a template such as that shown in Table 8.1 (or a similar template), we can start to sketch out a particular application of the ABCs for a particular topic. The template can be expanded to include the tools and techniques we have discussed in this book.

Building a security culture

There is still one question or point I haven't addressed. How can we build the 'security culture' we all, as cybersecurity professionals, believe to be critical to protecting organisational information?

The answer is: we can't.[112]

What you can build, with some success, is twofold: first you can introduce and integrate security into the current culture; second you can build a security sub-culture in one or more defined groups of people.

The first point of success, introducing and integrating security into the current culture, relies heavily on understanding the organisational culture and injecting symbols, artefacts and stories into the cultural milieu. Security champions and 'satisfied customers' can be just as useful as senior executives in telling stories, setting out acceptable behaviours and reinforcing 'the way we do things around here'. These individuals can, through personal example and action, bring cybersecurity to the desk and make it a living, real thing, rather than a dry, slideware subject. These individuals also help us to beat the numbers game mentioned earlier; in large organisations, the cybersecurity function can't be physically present much of the time (there are just too many things to do!), so these individuals extend our reach, extend our influence and provide a point of presence in a way we can't do ourselves. Time spent working with these individuals can introduce stories, behaviours and norms into the workplace that help to enrich and change the culture in small, yet meaningful ways.

There is much the security function can do as well. Obviously, having been through our ABCs and delivering those positive moments of truth and behaviours, we'll be much more integrated into the culture ourselves. This should allow us to design and use the right stories and artefacts, alongside our presentations, to enrich and change the culture as we'll be using the norms, the language and the approach recognised by the culture. Importantly we can then back those changes with our behaviours.

Just because it's very difficult to change the culture as a whole, it doesn't mean you can't change a sub-culture, our second point of success. Organisational culture is made up of many things and there may be sub-cultures centred on certain departments or functions. One of these departments or functions may have a security or data 'consciousness', in that they handle sensitive data or work with particular clients who require information to be protected. These functions may already have a security culture in some sense and can be very fertile ground for the creation of a cybersecurity culture. Applying the ABCs and working with the individuals in the team to define and then create change through tailored messages and activities should embed security further into the sub-culture and help the team to raise their game (or ensure they don't slip back). Such an approach focuses cybersecurity resources to protect sensitive information and positions cybersecurity nicely as the team who helped.

FINAL THOUGHTS

There is no magic bullet in cybersecurity, however much we as security professionals wish there was. Despite our increasing reliance on technology and information in all its forms, the overall level of education about technology and security is still very low.

Organisations and cybersecurity professionals are faced with this lack of understanding and are compelled to address it. Security awareness is the key tool we have to deal with this lack of understanding, yet it is imperfect for many reasons.

Our perspective – and one we have set out in this book – is that we can improve security awareness and other related initiatives by taking a step back and considering not just the narrow 'issue of the day' but the context – the culture and behaviours of an organisation – in which awareness is used and in which we try to provide education, training and activities to perform.

The ABCs are very much a people-driven approach. People are still the biggest issue and the biggest solution we have. Not to approach cybersecurity from their perspective is to deny ourselves one of the key success factors we have.

POSTSCRIPT

Adrian Davis

Much of this book was written before the COVID-19 pandemic swept across the globe in 2020. At a time when many organisations have the majority of their staff working from home and social distancing is the norm, the concepts we have discussed here – security awareness, behaviours and organisational cultures – can seem disconnected from the reality we are experiencing at the time of writing and the cybersecurity challenges we face.

However, these concepts are more meaningful than ever. As individuals come to terms with working from home using new IT, new software and becoming more reliant on their own judgement when it comes to cybersecurity, the ABCs assume a new and more important role. For many individuals, if they click on a link or download a free app from the internet, they may find their sole source of work and income – their IT – is taken away from them. There is no IT department to call for help or someone who can 'pop up and take a look'; such help is delivered remotely, through the very IT that has just been compromised through their actions. Cybersecurity incidents are no longer someone else's or the business' problem. Incidents are personal.

Remote working throws up a number of challenges, but there are many technical solutions that can be implemented to provide a reasonable level of protection to remote IT equipment. But aside from the technology, the only other level of protection we have is the individual: what they can remember from awareness training, the habits and behaviours they have adopted (or adapted) when working from home, the habits and behaviours they remember from the office and their judgement. In sum, the bits of the organisational culture they remember and apply when they sit down in front of their laptops.

Organisational culture[113] can be a strong influencer as people adopt to the different ways of working that are now being practised, as it can give them a sense of belonging, a sense of normality and guidance on their work behaviour outside their usual work environments. We can build on those remembered behaviours, through clear and simple messaging. Whereas our audience for culture change was the team, function or organisation, we know now it also has to be the individual or the small group. Our messages have to become less formal, less 'do not' and much more engaging, more about 'how to' and, in some senses, 'carry on'.

And that is what we suggest you do: carry on. Use the guidance, tools and insights we have presented here to help you improve people's knowledge, behaviours and judgements through the ABCs.

NOTES

1   Tversky and Kahneman, 1973; https://thedecisionlab.com/biases/availability-heuristic/

2   Adapted from NIST SP800-16.

3   https://www.ncsc.gov.uk/files/Business-email-compromise-infographic.pdf

4   https://www.behavioraleconomics.com/resources/mini-encyclopedia-of-be/choice-architecture/

5   https://www.psychologytoday.com/us/basics/cognitive-dissonance

6   In addition, other properties, such as authenticity, accountability, non-repudiation, and reliability can also be involved.

7   Adapted from the definition for information security in ISO/IEC 27000:2009 (ISO/IEC 27032:2012, retrieved using www.iso.org/obp).

8   https://www.lexico.com/ definition/cybersecurity

9   Cygenta.

10   ISO/IEC 27032:2012, retrieved using www.iso.org/obp

11   https://www.themantic-education.com/ibpsych/2016/10/24/single-and-double-blind-designs/

12   Kruger and Dunning, 1999.

13   https://dictionary.cambridge.org/dictionary/english/gamification

14   Kerr, 1998, https://doi.org/10.1207/s15327957pspr0203_4

15   https://opentextbc.ca/businessopenstax/chapter/the-hawthorne-studies/

16   https://www.psychologytoday.com/us/basics/heuristics

17   https://dictionary.cambridge.org/dictionary/english/norm

18   Drabek, 1986.

19   https://www.behavioraleconomics.com/resources/mini-encyclopedia-of-be/nudge/

20   https://psychologydictionary.org/null-hypothesis/

21   Skinner, 1948.

22   https://dictionary.cambridge.org/dictionary/english/pedagogy

23   Phishing can be accomplished by using social engineering or technical deception. ISO/IEC 27032:2012, retrieved using www.iso.org/obp

24   Ajzen, 1991 and https://sphweb.bumc.bu.edu/otlt/MPH-Modules/SB/BehavioralChangeTheories/BehavioralChangeTheories3.html

25   Rogers, 1975.

26   https://www.enisa.europa.eu/topics/csirts-in-europe/glossary/ransomware

27   https://thedecisionlab.com/salience-bias/

28   Bandura, 1995.

29   Cialdini, 2007.

30   https://www.enisa.europa.eu/topics/csirts-in-europe/glossary/phishing-spear-phishing

31   Adapted from NIST SP800-16.

32   https://www.sans.org/security-awareness-training/resources/two-step-verification

33   It is also the third highest information security-related search in Google Scholar.

34   https://www.theregister.co.uk/2007/04/17/chocolate_password_survey/. See also: https://youtu.be/opRMrEfAliI and https://www.youtube.com/watch?v=UzvPP6_LRHc. In both cases these are the same activity repeated a couple of years apart; yet the same results.

35   See for example: https://money.cnn.com/2015/08/22/technology/ashley-madison-hack-government-workers/index.html

36   See https://geerthofstede.com/ and https://www.hofstede-insights.com/. Geert Hofstede died in February 2020.

37   SP800-16 is now relegated to the NIST 'legacy' list along with SP800-50. Both, however, contain a wealth of useful information on cybersecurity awareness, training and education.

38   In fact, placing awareness messages or posters in toilets seems to be a very popular approach. I've seen such messages in the toilet facilities of many organisations, including banks, catering organisations and consultancies.

39   As Douglas Adams put it in *So Long, and Thanks for All the Fish*: 'a very respectable view widely held by right-thinking people, who are largely recognizable as being right-thinking people by the mere fact that they hold this view'.

40   As first noted by Irving Janis in his 1972 study.

41   I've stolen Jess's headline and probably her thunder here – sorry Jess!

42   An experiment in Amsterdam railway station swapped the till displays from chocolate to fruit and registered an increase in sales of fruit: https://academic.oup.com/jpubhealth/article/38/2/e133/2241365

43   Other examples are at: https://medium.com/swlh/the-7-most-creative-examples-of-habit-changing-nudges-7873ca1fff4a

44 https://bthechange.com/organizational-change-failures-what-happened-to-daimlerchrysler-and-aol-time-warner-ff2b2c8fcb0e provides examples of failures where culture change didn't happen.

45 https://blog.cygenta.co.uk/2fa_2019/

46 https://www.ncsc.gov.uk/speech/people--the-strongest-link

47 https://blogs.ucl.ac.uk/digital-education/2014/02/04/learning-on-steroids-with-richard-feynman/

48 https://www.sans.org/security-awareness-training/blog/accelerated-learning-european-secawaresummit

49 The last two questions are also linked to the organisational culture, of which more later.

50 https://www.ncsc.gov.uk/collection/passwords?curPage=/collection/passwords/updating-your-approach and https://pages.nist.gov/800-63-3/sp800-63b.html#memsecretver

51 These numbers are sourced from: https://www.forbes.com/sites/louiscolumbus/2020/04/05/2020-roundup-of-cybersecurity-forecasts-and-market-estimates/

52 A review, published in 1952, found over 134 definitions – and took 219 pages to review and classify them. See https://www.journals.uchicago.edu/doi/pdf/10.1086/221402 and Kroeber and Kluckhohn (1952, pp. viii, 223).

53 See for example: https://hbr.org/2013/05/what-is-organizational-culture

54 Or, even worse, doing both.

55 The *Harvard Business Review* article (https://hbr.org/2013/05/what-is-organizational-culture) contains a number of definitions similar to – and different from – the definitions presented here.

56 See: https://geerthofstede.com/landing-page/

57 See https://hi.hofstede-insights.com/national-culture and https://geerthofstede.com/culture-geert-hofstede-gert-jan-hofstede/6d-model-of-national-culture/

58 The highest level of Maslow's Hierarchy of Needs: https://www.explorepsychology.com/maslows-hierarchy-of-needs/ and http://psychclassics.yorku.ca/Maslow/motivation.htm

59 https://sloanreview.mit.edu/article/coming-to-a-new-awareness-of-organizational-culture/?use_credit=fecf2c550171d3195c879d115440ae45

60 Neatly summarised by Sidney Yoshida (1989).

61 See https://www.psychologytoday.com/us/basics/cognitive-dissonance

62 See Chapter 5 for a great example of habit forming – locking computers.

63 DLA Piper GDPR Data Breach Survey 2020: https://www.dlapiper.com/en/uk/insights/publications/2020/01/gdpr-data-breach-survey-2020/

64 As defined by 'Homo economicus': https://www.behavioraleconomics.com/resources/mini-encyclopedia-of-be/homo-economicus/

65   Nudge theory, which we discussed in Chapter 1.

66   Popularised in his book *Thinking Fast and Slow* (Kahneman, 2011).

67   A simple test to show the difference is as follows; multiply 2 × 2, 20 × 20 and then 17 × 24 without using a calculator. The last multiplication triggers System 2 thinking for most non-mathematicians, or a heuristic answer.

68   https://www.psychologistworld.com/influence/social-influence

69   Examples of top down change include: https://www.forbes.com/sites/grantfreeland/2018/07/16/culture-change-it-starts-at-the-top/ and Johnson and Scholes' case study of change in KPMG (Johnson et al., 2012).

70   https://www.forbes.com/sites/forbesbusinesscouncil/2019/11/21/building-culture-from-the-top-down/

71   https://www.fca.org.uk/news/speeches/getting-culture-and-conduct-right-role-regulator

72   For example: https://othjournal.com/2018/06/18/innovation-from-the-bottom-up-how-design-thinking-can-transform-the-air-force-culture/ and https://www.forbes.com/sites/forbescoachescouncil/2018/10/17/how-to-empower-a-bottom-up-culture-in-your-company/

73   From Thaler and Sunstein (2009), Thaler et al. (2013) and https://www.sas.upenn.edu/~baron/475/choice.architecture.pdf

74   Configuring everyone's laptop with automatic encryption is a good example. The owner never has to think about it and a level of security is automatically integrated into their normal workplace behaviour.

75   See https://hbr.org/2020/04/build-a-culture-that-aligns-with-peoples-values

76   See https://knowledge.insead.edu/strategy/culture-can-make-or-break-strategy-3730 and https://www.torbenrick.eu/blog/strategy/relationship-between-culture-and-strategy/

77   For example https://www.torbenrick.eu/blog/culture/dark-side-of-coporate-culture/ and https://www.torbenrick.eu/blog/culture/corporate-cultures-breed-dishonesty/ for good summaries.

78   To put our contribution into perspective, a search on Google Scholar for corporate culture change and organisational culture change produces about 5 million results in total.

79   'Culture comes from the past': https://www.fca.org.uk/news/speeches/getting-culture-and-conduct-right-role-regulator

80   See https://www.kotterinc.com/8-steps-process-for-leading-change/. Schein also has a model for culture change, see for example: https://sites.psu.edu/global/2020/04/07/managing-organizational-change-lewin-schein/

81   Without diving into the politics, the #MeToo and Black Lives Matter campaigns are also visible reactions to toxic cultures in our four types (macro, organisational, sub and micro) and found in many institutions and organisations.

82   https://www.fca.org.uk/news/speeches/our-approach-cyber-security-financial-services-firms

83   https://hbr.org/2016/12/how-to-discover-your-companys-dna and https://www.torbenrick.eu/blog/culture/organizational-culture-needs-to-change-fundamentally/; see the quote from Sony.

84   https://hbswk.hbs.edu/archive/gerstner-changing-culture-at-ibm-lou-gerstner-discusses-changing-the-culture-at-ibm

85   Schein (2009) has some powerful examples in *The Corporate Culture Survival Guide*.

86   Slightly dated, but this is a great study of a strong culture and the efforts to change it: https://www.forbes.com/sites/stevedenning/2011/07/23/how-do-you-change-an-organizational-culture/

87   https://angelareddix.com/leadership/how-to-build-a-strong-organizational-culture/, https://www.forbes.com/sites/nazbeheshti/2018/09/17/3-strategies-to-build-a-strong-company-culture/ and https://www.shrm.org/Resources AndTools/tools-and-samples/toolkits/Pages/understandinganddeveloping organizationalculture.aspx

88   https://hbr.org/2019/12/to-build-a-strong-culture-create-rules-that-are-unique-to-your-company

89   https://www.forbes.com/sites/davidrock/2019/05/24/fastest-way-to-change-culture/

90   https://www.forbes.com/sites/grantfreeland/2018/07/16/culture-change-it-starts-at-the-top/ is a very good case study of how changing board behaviours and focus can help to create the desired culture change.

91   I find it annoying that investment as a noun is hijacked by continual association to money.

92   Without straying into the field of organisational decision-making, it is worth remembering that many decisions are agreed before formal meetings (at any level). The formal meeting and decision merely confirm to a wider audience the decision that has been made.

93   Wikipedia has a list of 117 belief, decision-making and behavioural biases: https://en.wikipedia.org/wiki/List_of_cognitive_biases; see also: https://medium.com/better-humans/cognitive-bias-cheat-sheet-55a472476b18#.ltfki4836

94   Taylor and Fiske (1975) and https://thedecisionlab.com/biases/salience-bias/

95   'The initial response to a disaster warning is disbelief' (Drabek, 1986, p. 72).

96   Or, 'No plan survives contact with the enemy', attributed to Graf Helmuth von Moltke the elder: 'Kein Plan überlebt die erste Feindberührung'.

97   https://www.theatlantic.com/business/archive/2017/10/money-measure-everything-pricing-progress/543345/

98   For example: https://cybersecurity.att.com/blogs/security-essentials/how-to-justify-your-cybersecurity-budget

99   As an example, insert the name of any pop musician or celebrity since 1950!

100 https://www.mas.gov.sg/publications/monographs-or-information-paper/2020/information-paper-on-culture-and-conduct-practices-of-financial-institutions; see Outcome 5 and 8.

101 In one such discussion, a cybersecurity professional told me, 'I should be paid more than the entire board because I produce miracles with no money, no team and no support.' I suppose it's a matter of culture.

102 An obvious statement but one worth repeating: labour and employment laws and cultures differ around the world.

103 See for example: https://www.peoplemanagement.co.uk/voices/comment/has-your-organisation-turned-into-a-monoculture

104 Tools such as the Feynman technique can use and reinforce these stories.

105 A fellow cybersecurity professional once told me, 'I would rather stick pins in my eyes than read another [cyber] security policy'.

106 https://www.iso.org/isoiec-27001-information-security.html

107 Download at: https://www.nist.gov/cyberframework

108 Download at: https://www.pcisecuritystandards.org/document_library

109 AIDA is attributed to E. St Elmo Lewis: https://www.oxfordreference.com/view/10.1093/oi/authority.20110803095432783

110 Scandinavian Air Systems, not the UK military's Special Air Service.

111 The distance from Marathon to Athens, covered by the Athenian Army in full battle armour after the battle of Marathon to head off a further Persian landing nearer to Athens: 25 miles. In other words, a long and difficult journey, with the prospect of further battle at the end of it.

112 OK, you as the reader can say that I am being very negative and that, actually, you can build a security culture in certain types of organisations, such as cybersecurity companies, small to medium-sized organisations, start-ups where the culture is being formed or the business is cybersecurity, and organisations that have been through a major information security incident. Read on.

113 https://www.forbes.com/sites/tracybrower/2020/05/25/how-to-sustain-and-strengthen-company-culture-through-the-coronavirus-pandemic/

BIBLIOGRAPHY

Ajzen, I. (1991) The theory of planned behavior. *Organizational Behavior and Human Decision Processes*, *50*(2), 179–211.

Arkalgud, U. and Partridge, J. (2020) *Microcultures*, Lulu Publishing Services.

Ashenden, D. and Sasse, A. (2013) CISOs and organisational culture: Their own worst enemy? *Computers & Security, 39*, 396–405. http://doi.org/10.1016/j.cose.2013.09.004

Babad, E. Y., Inbar, J. and Rosenthal, R. (1982) Pygmalion, Galatea, and the Golem: Investigations of biased and unbiased teachers. *Journal of Educational Psychology, 74*(4), 459–474.

Bada, M., Sasse, A. M. and Nurse, J. R. C. (2015) Cyber security awareness campaigns: Why do they fail to change behaviour? In *International Conference on Cybersecurity for Sustainable Society*, Coventry University, 26–27 February 2015, pp. 118–131. Sustainable Society Network.

Bandura, A. (1971) *Social Learning Theory*, General Learning Press, New York.

Bandura, A. (1995) Self-efficacy. In A. S. R. Manstead and M. Hewstone (Eds), *Blackwell Encyclopedia of Social Psychology* (pp. 453–454), Blackwell, Oxford.

Beyer, M., Ahmed, S., Doerlemann, K., Arnell, S., Parkin, S., Sasse, A. M. and Passingham, S. (2015) *Awareness is Only the First Step: A Framework for Progressive Engagement of Staff in Cybersecurity*, Hewlett-Packard Enterprise. https://www.riscs.org.uk/wp-content/uploads/2015/12/Awareness-is-Only-the-First-Step.pdf

Bulgurcu, B., Cavusoglu, H. and Benbasat, I. (2009) Roles of information security awareness and perceived fairness in information security policy compliance. In *15th Americas Conference on Information Systems*, Vol. 5, San Francisco, 6–9 August, pp. 3269–3277. Association for Information Systems.

Carella, A., Kotsoev, M. and Truta, T. M. (2017) Impact of security awareness training on phishing click-through rates. In *2017 IEEE International Conference on Big Data (Big Data)*, Boston, MA, 11–14 December, Vol. 2018, pp. 4458–4466. IEEE. https://doi.org/10.1109/BigData.2017.8258485

Carlzon, J. (1987) *Moments of Truth*, Ballinger Publishing Company, Cambridge.

Cialdini, R. B. (2007) *Influence: The Psychology of Persuasion*, Harper Collins, New York.

ClubCISO (2020) Information Security Maturity Report 2020: Full Survey Results [Online] https://www.clubciso.org/downloads/

Coventry, L., Briggs, P., Blythe, J. and Tran, M. (2014) *Summary Report: Using Behavioural Insights to Improve the Public's Use of Cybersecurity Best Practices*, Government Office for Science, London.

Cyber Security Policy (2018) *Securing Cyber Resilience in Health and Care: Progress Update October 2018*, Department of Health and Social Care. https://assets.publishing. service.gov.uk/government/uploads/system/uploads/attachment_data/file/747464/ securing-cyber-resilience-in-health-and-care-september-2018-update.pdf

Drabek, T. E. (1986) *Human System Responses to Disaster: An Inventory of Sociological Findings*, Springer Verlag, New York.

Fox, K. (2014) *Watching the English*, revised edition, Hodder and Stoughton, London.

Hammerich, K. and Lewis, R. (2013) *Fish Can't See Water*, John Wiley & Sons, Chichester, UK.

Hofstede, G., Pedersen, P. B. and Hofstede, G. J. (2002) *Exploring Culture*, Intercultural Press, Yarmouth, ME.

Hofstede, G., Hofstede, G. J. and Minkov, M. (2010) *Cultures and Organisations*, McGraw Hill, New York.

Information Security Forum (2020) *The Standard of Good Practice for Information Security 2020*, Information Security Forum, London.

International Standards Organisation (2013) ISO/IEC 27001:2013, Information technology – Security techniques – Information security management system – Requirements. https://www.iso.org/standard/54534.html

International Standards Organisation (2017) ISO/IEC 27021:2017, Information technology – Security techniques – Competence requirements for information security management systems professionals. https://www.iso.org/standard/61003.html

Janis, I. (1972) *Victims of Groupthink: A Psychological Study of Foreign-Policy Decisions and Fiascoes*, Houghton Mifflin, Boston, MA.

Johnson, G., Whittington, R. and Scholes, K. (2012) *Fundamentals of Strategy*, Pearson Education, London.

Kahneman, D. (2011) *Thinking Fast and Slow*, Penguin, London.

Kemp, S. (2004) Planning behaviour: A re-examination of the organisational culture present in the Regent International Hotels' Group. *International Journal of Applied Strategic Management*, 2(1), 1–19. www.managementjournals.com/journals/strategic/vol2/12-2-1-1.pdf

Kerr, N. L. (1998) HARKing: Hypothesizing after the results are known. *Personality and Social Psychology Review*, 2(3), 196–217.

Kotter, J. P. (2012) *Leading Change*, Harvard Business Review Press, Boston, MA.

Kralik, J. D., Xu, E. R., Knight, E. J., Khan, S. A. and Levine, W. J. (2012) When less is more: Evolutionary origins of the affect heuristic. *PLoS ONE*, 7(10), e46240. https://doi.org/10.1371/journal.pone.0046240

Kroeber, A. L. and Kluckhohn, C. (1952) Culture: A critical review of concepts and definitions. *Papers of the Peabody Museum of Archaeology and Ethnology, Harvard University*, vol. 47, no. 1. Peabody Museum of Archaeology and Ethnology, Cambridge, MA.

Kruger, J. and Dunning, D. (1999) Unskilled and unaware of it: How difficulties in recognizing one's own incompetence lead to inflated self-assessments. *Journal of Personality and Social Psychology, 77*(6), 1121–1134.

Kruger, J., Wirtz, D., Van Boven, L. and Altermatt, T. W. (2004) The effort heuristic. *Journal of Experimental Social Psychology, 40*(1), 91–98. https://doi.org/10.1016/S0022-1031(03)00065-9

Leventhal, H., Singer, R. and Jones, S. (1965) Effects of fear and specificity of recommendation upon attitudes and behavior. *Journal of Personality and Social Psychology, 2*(1), 20–29.

Meier, D. (2000) *The Accelerated Learning Handbook: A Creative Guide to Designing and Delivering Faster, More Effective Training Programs*, McGraw-Hill, New York.

Monetary Authority of Singapore (MAS) (2020) *Information Paper on Culture and Conduct Practices of Financial Institutions*. https://www.mas.gov.sg/publications/monographs-or-information-paper/2020/information-paper-on-culture-and-conduct-practices-of-financial-institutions

National Institute of Science and Technology (2003) SP 800-50 Building an information technology security awareness and training program. https://csrc.nist.gov/publications/detail/sp/800-50/final

Padayachee, K. (2012) Taxonomy of compliant information security behavior. *Computers & Security, 31*(5), 673–680. https://doi.org/10.1016/j.cose.2012.04.004

Parsons, K., McCormac, A., Butavicius, M., Pattinson, M. and Jerram, C. (2014) Determining employee awareness using the Human Aspects of Information Security Questionnaire (HAIS-Q). *Computers & Security, 42*, 165–176. https://doi.org/10.1016/j.cose.2013.12.003

Pilar, D. R., Jaeger, A., Gomes, C. F. A. and Stein, L. M. (2012) Passwords usage and human memory limitations: A survey across age and educational background. *PloS One, 7*(12), e51067. http://doi.org/10.1371/journal.pone.0051067

Rogers, R. W. (1975) A protection motivation theory of fear appeals and attitude change. *The Journal of Psychology, 91*(1), 93–114. https://doi.org/10.1080/00223980.1975.9915803

Ruiter, R. A. C. (2014) Sixty years of fear appeal research: Current state of the evidence. *International Journal of Psychology, 49*(2), 67.

Schein, E. H. (1985) *Organizational Culture and Leadership: A Dynamic View*, Jossey-Bass, San Francisco.

Schein, E. H. (2009) *The Corporate Culture Survival Guide*, 2nd edition, Jossey-Bass, San Francisco.

Schein, E. H. (2016) *Organizational Culture and Leadership*, 5th edition, John Wiley & Sons, Hoboken, NJ.

Sinek, S. (2011) *Start with Why: How Great Leaders Inspire Everyone to Take Action*, Penguin, London.

Skinner, B. F. (1948) 'Superstition' in the pigeon. *Journal of Experimental Psychology, 38*(2), 168–172.

Stanton, B., Theofanos, M. F., Prettyman, S. S. and Furman, S. (2016) Security fatigue. *IT Professional*, Sep–Oct 2016.

Stewart, J. M., Chapple, M. and Gibson, G. (2015) *CISSP (ISC)² Certified Information Systems Security Professional Official Study Guide*, 7th edition, John Wiley & Sons, Chichester.

Taylor, S. E. and Fiske, S. T. (1975) Point of view and perceptions of causality. *Journal of Personality and Social Psychology, 32*(3), 439–445. https://doi.org/10.1037/h0077095

Thaler, R. H. and Sunstein, C. R. (2009) *Nudge: Improving Decisions about Health, Wealth and Happiness*, Penguin, London.

Thaler, R. H., Sunstein, C. R. and Balz, J. P. (2013) Choice architecture. In E. Shafir (Ed.), *The Behavioral Foundations of Public Policy* (pp. 428–439), Princeton University Press, Princeton, NJ.

Thomson, M. E. and von Solms R. (1998) Information security awareness: Educating your users effectively. *Information Management & Computer Security, 6*(4), 167–173.

Tischer, M., Durumeric, Z., Foster, S., Duan, S., Mori, A., Bursztein, E. and Bailey, M. (2016) Users really do plug in USB drives they find. In *IEEE Symposium on Security and Privacy*, San Jose, CA, 22–26 May, 306–319. IEEE. http://doi.org/10.1109/SP.2016.26

Tversky, A. and Kahneman, D. (1973) Availability: A heuristic for judging frequency and probability. *Cognitive Psychology, 5*(2), 207–232. http://doi.org/10.1016/0010-0285(73)90033-9

Van Oudenhoven, J. P. (2001) Do organizations reflect national cultures? A 10-nation study. *International Journal of Intercultural Relations, 25*(1), 89–107. http://doi.org/10.1016/S0147-1767(00)00044-4

Verizon (2020) Data Breach Investigations Report [Online] https://enterprise.verizon.com/resources/reports/2020/2020-data-breach-investigations-report.pdf

Whitty, M. T., Doodson, J., Creese, S. and Hodges, D. (2015) Individual differences in cybersecurity behaviors: An examination of who is sharing passwords. *Cyberpsychology, Behavior, and Social Networking, 18*, 3–7. http://doi.org/10.1089/cyber.2014.0179

Witte, K. (1992) Putting the fear back into fear appeals: The extended parallel process model. *Communication Monographs, 59*(4), 329–349.

Witte, K. and Alen, M. (2000) A meta-analysis of fear appeals: Implications for effective public health campaigns. *Health Education & Behavior, 27*, 591–615.

Yeats, W. B. (1920) *Michael Robartes and the Dancer*, Cuala Press, Dublin.

Yoshida, S. (1989) The iceberg of ignorance. In *International Quality Symposium,* Mexico City, Mexico.

INDEX